GEM TRAILS
OF
CALIFORNIA

By James R. Mitchell

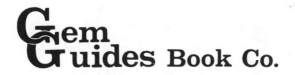

Gem Guides Book Co.

3677 San Gabriel River Parkway
Pico Rivera, CA 90660

Copyright © 1986

GEM GUIDES BOOK CO.

First Edition, 1972
Second Edition, 1978
Third Edition, 1986

All rights reserved. This book may not be reproduced in any form without the written permission of the publisher.

Library of Congress Catalog Card Number 78-187288

ISBN 0-935182-22-5

Maps by JOHN N. MAYERSKI

Note: Due to the possibilities of misinterpretation of information, *Gem Trails of California*, its author, publisher and all other persons directly and indirectly involved with this publication assume no responsibility for accidents, injury or any losses by individuals or groups using this publication.

In rough terrain and hazardous areas all persons are advised to be aware of possible changes due to man or nature that can occur along the gem trails.

TABLE OF CONTENTS

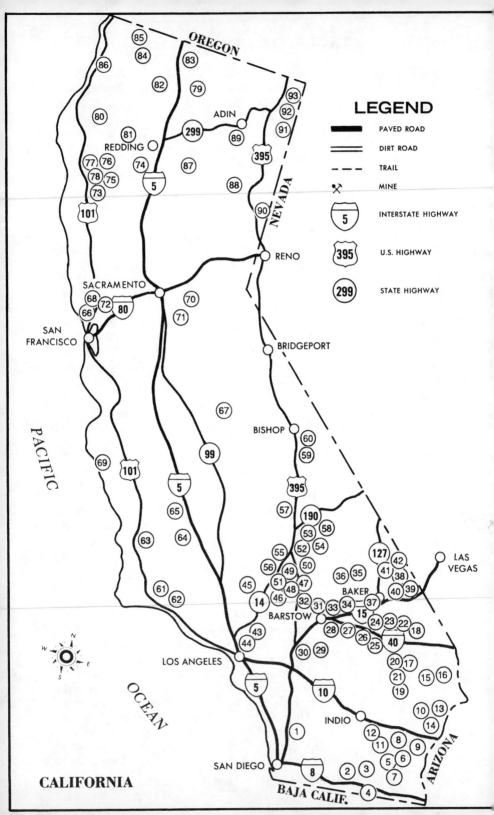

LOCATIONS

5

INTRODUCTION

California is well known for its beautiful gemstones and minerals. Rockhounds come from all over the world to explore the scenic state, searching for its mineral treasures. The supply seems limitless and, best of all, many of the prime collecting sites are situated on public lands. Probably no other part of the country offers better accessibility and variety than California.

Each of the locations listed in the revised "Gem Trails of California" was checked shortly before publication to verify mineral availability and that collecting was allowed. A few of the spots are privately owned and a fee is charged. That information is noted in the text. However, do not assume that this guide gives permission to collect! Land status changes frequently. If you have a suspicion that a particular site is no longer open to collectors, be sure to check the status before proceeding. If nothing can be determined locally, land ownership information is available at the County Recorder's office.

Most of the areas discussed on the following pages are easy to get to, but road conditions can change. Severe weather can make good roads very rough and very rough roads impassable, even with four-wheel drive. Do not attempt traveling where your vehicle was not designed to go.

The sites are situated in landscapes as full of variety as the minerals themselves. The terrrain varies from arid deserts to lofty snow-covered mountains. Because of these immense differences, do some advance research on the area you plan to visit. Don't take a trip to the desert during the sweltering summer months or to the high mountains during the winter. Doing so could not only result in an unpleasant trip, but could be dangerous.

When venturing into some of the more remote areas it is a good idea to take extra drinking water, foul weather clothing and, possibly, some food, just in case you get delayed or stuck. I am certain if you take some time to plan your collecting trip properly and make sure your vehicle is in good working order, the gem fields listed on the following pages will provide you and your family with outstanding minerals and many memorable experiences.

James R. Mitchell

PALA

This site is only open on weekends to people paying a fee to cover insurance and guide costs. It is one of the world's foremost tourmaline locations and a visit is well worth the small cost. To register for a Saturday or Sunday collecting trip, contact Johnny Springer (619) 722-2783 any weekday, between 8 and 10 a.m., or write to her at P.O. Box 23, Bonsall, CA 92003. Be sure to make reservations at least five days in advance.

The group meets at 10 a.m. at Gems of Pala, as shown on the map, and then travels together to the Stewart Lithia Mine. You will return at approximately 2 p.m. In addition to digging and rock splitting tools, it is suggested that visitors also take a flashlight, since it is often possible to enter one of the shafts and actually see a few gem pockets. You can dig into the dumps with small tools and keep anything you find, which often includes gem tourmaline crystals and beautiful lavender chunks of lepidolite. The tourmaline occurs in a rainbow of colors, including pink, blue, green, black, bicolored and watermelon. Each member of the party is allowed to take home 10 pounds of material.

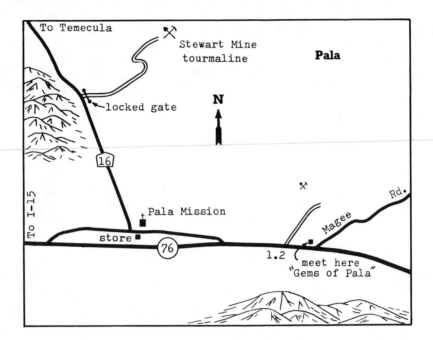

The Stewart Lithia Mine

From the Desk of . . . . .

JAMES A. MacRILL, M.D.

PHONE: 426-8376

ANZA-BORREGO

Nice selinite slabs can be found throughout the sand hills at Site A. They are bright white and, therefore, easily spotted, contrasting sharply with the brown sand. It takes very little work to remove a number of specimens. Simply dig into the soft soil with a hand rake or trowel wherever you happen to see the slabs. In addition to mineral collecting, the view from the sand hills affords a spectacular desert panorama.

To get to Site B, Shell Canyon, simply continue along the road, as shown on the map, through the wash. Be very careful not to get stuck in the loose sand though. If your vehicle is not capable of traveling on such terrain it is suggested that you hike rather than chance getting stuck. The canyon is filled with fossil shells and onyx, with the latter generally being white, light pink and green. Gads, chisels and sledge hammers are necessary to free the material from the walls, but such work can usually be avoided by simply examining the rocks and boulders lying in the washes and lowlands throughout the canyon.

Painted Gorge, Site C, offers more fossils as well as some scattered agate and jasper. This is regarded as one of the most scenic regions of the Colorado Desert and a side trip into the colorful gorge is worth the time, even if you don't do any collecting. The agate and jasper are sparsely scattered throughout the region, primarily to the south, while the blocky, fossil-bearing rock can easily be seen crumbling from the hills and cliffs in the area shown on the map.

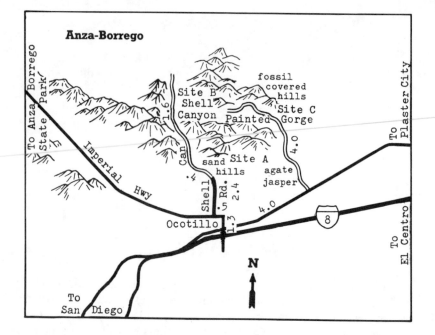

Anza-Borrego

To Anza Borrego State Park

Imperial Hwy

Shell Can

Site B
Shell
Canyon

sand
hills

Site A

Painted

fossil
covered
hills

Site C
Gorge

agate
jasper

1.6

.4

Rd.

.5

2.4

1.3

4.0

4.0

4.0

Ocotillo

8

To Plaster City

To El Centro

N

To San Diego

Fossil-covered hills in Painted Gorge, Site C

PLASTER CITY

The roads to both collecting areas are sandy, so you may have to walk part of the distance. Area A is extensive and noted for its well-formed petrified wood. Most pieces are small, but rains frequently expose large limb sections. The wood is randomly scattered throughout the hills and washes and patient searching is required. Once you find the first piece and see exactly what it looks like, however, subsequent specimens seem easier to find. Area B is a good place to find slabs of selenite. They are growing out of the sandstone cliffs shown on the map. It is difficult to find this site, since there are so many tracks throughout the region. Be patient, head in the proper direction, and you should have no major problem. Scant amounts of agate, jasper and chalcedony can also be found in this part of the desert.

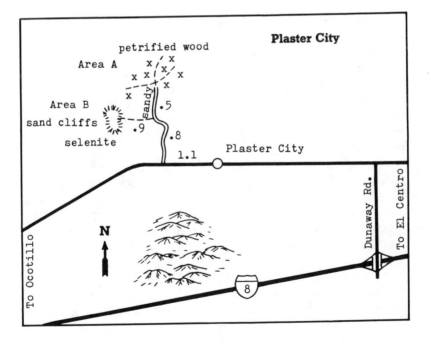

11

YUHA BASIN

These sites are only a short distance from Interstate 8 and offer the rockhound an opportunity to collect a variety of materials. It should be mentioned, though, that the roads cut through areas of clay, making them impassable when wet, even if in four-wheel drive.

To get to Site A, simply park off the ruts, at the given mileage, and hike south to the green and white hills. As you walk look for chalcedony, jasper, agate and obsidian. These gems are not overly plentiful, but some are quite colorful, making the search worthwhile. The hills at Site A are covered with rocks filled with fossil shells. It takes some time and patience to find the best specimens, but that extra effort is usually rewarded. You may want to do some pick and shovel work in order to uncover new and potentially better pieces.

At Site B, one can find unusual, spherical concretions in the areas surrounding the hill shown on the map. Just do some walking for quite a distance, keeping an eye to the ground. These unusual mineral oddities range from the size of marbles to a few that measure many feet across. Some look like dumbbells or cones but most are spheres. They are usually concentrically layered, making it easy to "repair" damaged ones by chipping off an outer layer to thereby form a perfect, but smaller, replica of the original.

Site C is another vast fossil area, similar to Site A, where nearly every hill is littered with fossil-filled rocks. In addition, one can find occasional selenite crystals growing in the soft soil. These crystals are fragile and should be handled with care.

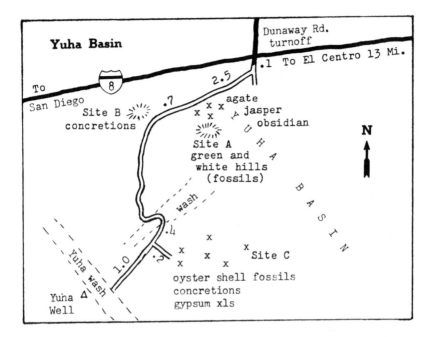

Yuha Basin

Dunaway Rd.
turnoff

To
San Diego

.1 To El Centro 13 Mi.

2.5

Site B
concretions

.7

agate
x x x
x x   jasper
obsidian

Site A
green and
white hills
(fossils)

Y U H A   B A S I N

N

wash

.4

x

.2   x   x   x   x   Site C

x   x   x

1.0

Yuha wash

oyster shell fossils
concretions
gypsum xls

Yuha
Well

Hill covered with oyster shell fossils

CHOCOLATE MOUNTAINS

The status of these sites is subject to change, so be certain the mines are inactive before doing any collecting. Site B, the old McKnight clay mine, is the primary area of interest. Here, one can find beautiful selenite crystals, some quite large. The fibrous selenite occurs in seams surrounding the quarry and chunks can also be found throughout the dump. Most are white, but some are red, green, pink and orange, and multi-colored pieces are the most highly prized. If you plan to attack the seams, it is helpful to have a heavy hammer and some gads, but the host rock and soil is quite soft so the work is not too difficult. Just be careful when climbing and working on the cliffs overlooking the quarry.

In addition to selenite, collectors can find small green fluorite crystals, brilliant white quartz, talc, calcite and a variety of uranium ores, including torbernite, autunite and carnotite.

Site A offers simlar minerals as can be found at Site B, but the quality and quantity are not so great.

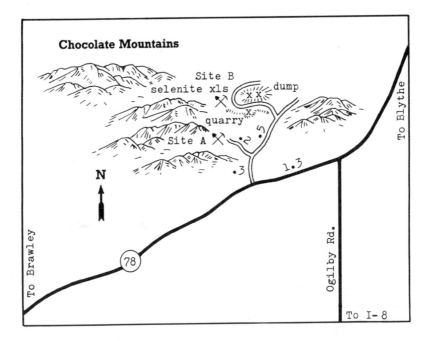

Chocolate Mountains

Site B
selenite xls

dump

quarry

Site A

N

78

To Brawley

To Blythe

Ogilby Rd.

To I-8

•2 •5

•3

1.3

McKnight clay mine dumps at Site B

GOLD BASIN

This part of the Colorado Desert is one of the most productive rockhounding regions in all of California. Collectors can unearth geodes ranging in size from very small to more than six inches across. It is easy to see where others have been digging, on both sides of the valley, and you can continue in these existing pits or start one of your own. The soil is soft making the work relatively easy, but a pick and shovel are essential. Many of the geodes are duds, but quite a few are filled with agate and/or beautiful crystals.

A little farther north of 78 you can pick up chalcedony, pastel green agate and colorful jasper, most of which is found in the region west of the hill near where you must park. More, however, can be obtained just about anywhere in the area. The deep gorge east of the road contains additional cutting materials, as well as hematite pebbles. In the brown hills and canyon west of the gorge look for calcite crystals filling cracks and cavities of the native rock. Nothing is overly plentiful and it takes patient searching to find worthwhile quantities.

In the terrain in and around the wash to the west of Midway Well agate can be found, as can chalcedony, rhyolite and bright red jasper. Areas surrounding the dark brown region about two hundred yards to the south offer better concentrations and rare pieces of fire agate. If you have time be sure to explore other nearby washes since most will contain similar minerals in varying quantities and qualities.

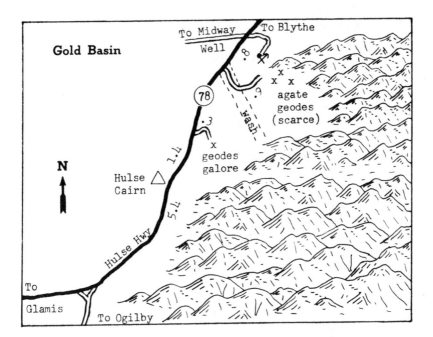

To Midway Well
To Blythe

Gold Basin

.8

x
x x
agate
geodes
(scarce)

78

.6

wash

N

.3

x
geodes
galore

Hulse
Cairn △

1.4

Hulse Hwy

5.4

To
Glamis

To Ogilby

Geodes

Parked at one of the geode diggings

17

CARGO MUCHACHO MOUNTAINS

Between 1925 and 1946 kyanite was removed from the Bluebird Mine, Site A, and shipped to Los Angeles for use in kilns and furnaces. Here at the now abandoned quarry, one can find outstanding blue kyanite crystals in bright white quartz. In addition, occasional limonite cubes can also be discovered. There is an active mine on the opposite side of the mountain and collecting is not allowed there. Site B is the famous Cargo Muchacho dumortierite location. Gem quality pieces of this beautiful blue material are getting very hard to find nowadays, but there still is a good amount of specimen grade chunks and boulders scattered throughout the hills and valleys. In addition, there is a lot of agate, petrified palm and jasper at Site B. Scarce amounts of agate and jasper can also be picked up at Site C.

Parked at kyanite location

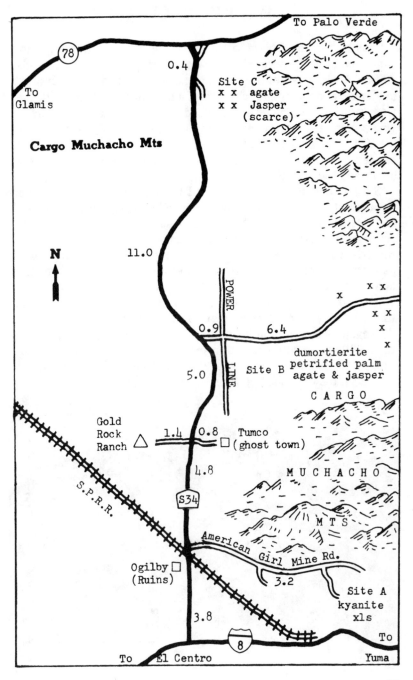

To Palo Verde

78

To Glamis

0.4

Site C
x x agate
x x Jasper
(scarce)

Cargo Muchacho Mts

N

11.0

POWER LINE

0.9   6.4   x   x x
                  x x
              x

5.0   Site B

dumortierite
petrified palm
agate & jasper

C A R G O

Gold
Rock   △   1.4   0.8   □ Tumco
Ranch   (ghost town)

4.8   M U C H A C H O

S34   M T S

S.P.R.R.

American Girl Mine Rd.

3.2

Ogilby □
(Ruins)

Site A
kyanite
xls

3.8

8   To

To   El Centro   Yuma

19

WILEY WELL

This part of the Colorado Desert has been productive for many years and still offers rockhounds an amazing variety of materials. At Site A a number of diggings can be seen on the hills north of the road extending about three-tenths of a mile from the given mileage. Here you can find agate and chalcedony. The road ends at Site B where more agate and chalcedony can be found. Follow the trail up the cliff for the best material. There are geodes, nodules and banded agate to be found at Site C, which consists of extensive upper and lower digging areas.

Sites D and E, Potato Patch and the Hauser Beds, are famous throughout the country for their spectacular agate-filled geodes and nodules, as well as lots of beautiful agate, jasper and chalcedony. Another extensive agate, geode and nodule location is Site F. Material can be found in the valley below the parking spot, as well as along the trail leading west around the mountain. The nodule and geode diggings at Site G can be seen from the road across the wash and you must hike the short distance to those somewhat limited excavations. Site H is an excellent agate and opalite spot. The agate occurs in seams on both sides of the upper ridges, while the opalite is on boulders and in seams on the lower eastern slopes. Site I is an extensive agate, geode and chalcedony locale. Be sure to follow all the trails leading from the parking area.

Famous Hauser Beds near Site E

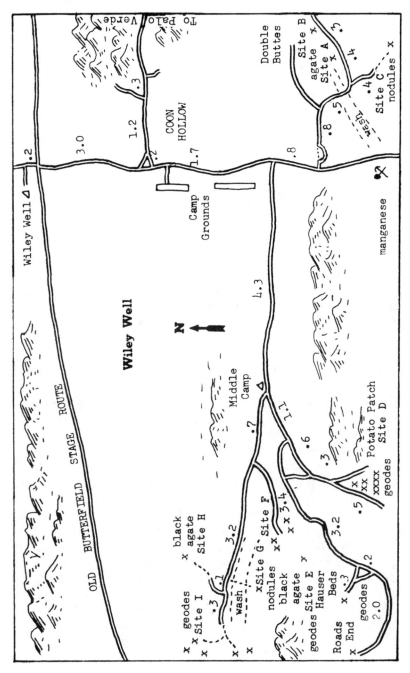

PALO VERDE (PEBBLE TERRACE)

Most of the desert pavement in this locality contains beautiful agate and jasper. Much, however, is concealed with a dark coating of desert varnish, making it necessary to split suspect stones to ascertain their true nature. The agate and jasper can be found throughout the flatlands, stretching west from Palo Verde to the foothills. The best concentrations, however, seem to start about three and four-tenths miles past the power lines, as shown on the map. Occasionally, petrified wood, chalcedony roses and fire agate can be obtained in the washes near the hills. The wood tends to be light brown, but some contains bright orange stringers, making it especially desirable. The roses are generally white, but many contain brown and orange swirls. The latter should be examined carefully for traces of fire.

Some of the finest fire agate to be found in California comes from the Opal Hill Mine, nestled deep in the Mule Mountains, about nine miles west of Palo Verde. A fee is charged to collect there, but nearly everybody who is willing to put forth some effort can find fire agate worth considerably more than the fee. It isn't easy to remove the fiery gemstones from their place in the hard host rock, and a sledge hammer, gads, and chisels are necessary pieces of equipment, as are goggles and a heavy pair of gloves. In addition, be sure to take something to drink, since working in this arid climate will make you thirsty. The mine is open from October 15 until May 1, and current information can be obtained by writing to the Opal Hill Mine, P.O. Box 232, Palo Verde, CA 92266 or by phoning (714) 922-6256, after 7 p.m. Reservations are not necessary.

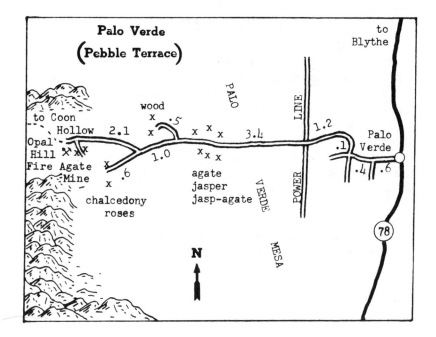

Palo Verde
(Pebble Terrace)

to Coon Hollow
Opal Hill Fire Agate Mine

wood
2.1   .5
1.0   .6
chalcedony roses

agate
jasper
jasp-agate

PALO

VERDE

MESA

POWER LINE

3.4   1.2
.1
.4   .6

to Blythe

Palo Verde

78

N

Many rocks in foreground are jasper and agate

23

BLYTHE

Unusual specimens of psilomelane can be collected at the old Arlington Manganese Mine. Look for the botryoidal pieces, which can be polished much like malachite to produce bull's-eyes or bands. The finest, however, should not be cut, since the velvet-black nodes make outstanding display pieces for mineral collections. The psilomelane can be found everywhere, and is easy to spot because of its jet black color. Crack any stone that appears somewhat porous; maybe you'll find mineral-bearing pockets or fissures. This takes lots of work, especially if you attack sizeable boulders, but the rewards are worth it. Be sure to also inspect the quarry itself. Psilomelane bearing seams can be seen criss-crossing the walls. Be careful, though, since the rock is somewhat crumbly, and pieces can fall from above.

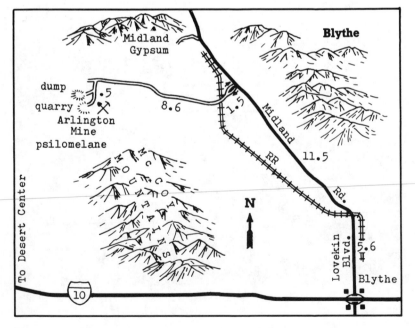

A fine specimen of botryoidal psilomelane

Parked near the old Arlington Manganese Mine

CHUCKAWALLA WELL

Agate, jasper and chalcedony can be found throughout the hills and valleys on both sides of the Old Butterfield Stage Route, starting about 10 miles west of the Wiley Well Campground and continuing approximately 15 miles farther. For the most part, the concentrations are random, making collecting somewhat frustrating. There are, however, two spots which, over the years, have proven to be particularly reliable. The first, labeled Site A on the accompanying map, boasts fine black agate, sagenite and occasional nodules and geodes. The excavations will be seen on the hillside as you approach the given mileage. To procure the best material, it is necessary to do some digging, but the work is relatively easy since the soil is soft. Most of the geodes and nodules are solid, having centers of banded agate, but a few do have crystalline interiors.

Chuckawalla Well, Site B, is approximately nine miles further west, and has long been known among rockhounds. Because of this publicity, however, much of the best surface material has already been taken. There is still plenty of agate, jasper and petrified wood available, if you are willing to do some hiking through the nearby hills and valleys. Just be patient and plan to spend some time. Material is most frequently found in areas of erosion, but it can also be picked up on the hillsides and even along the ruts leading in from the main road. Signs of digging can be seen on the hills to the north, and it is sometimes productive to do some work in those areas. Most of the seams, however, were worked out many years ago. DO NOT camp or park near Chuckawalla Well, since it is an important watering spot for local wildlife.

Chuckawalla Well

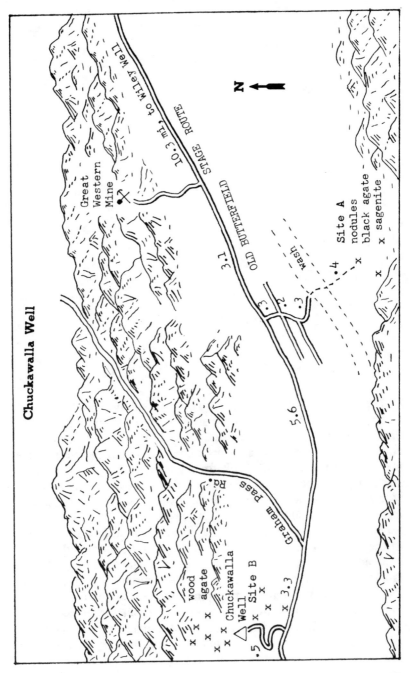

CHUCKAWALLA SPRING

These three Chuckawalla Spring sites have been worked extensively over the years, but there is still plenty to be found. At Site A, one can obtain agate and, every now and then, some nice nodules. These materials are now quite scarce, but patient searching is usually rewarded. Look for signs of digging as a place to start. A great deal of bubbly chalcedony has been found at Site B, but, as was the case at Site A, it is now necessary to walk a distance from the road to have much success.

The hills above Chuckawalla Spring and the road leading through the wash west of the spring are loaded with agate, chalcedony, chert and occasional geodes and nodules. This is labeled Site C on the map, and is the most productive of the three. Don't get stuck driving through the sandy wash, though.

There was a collecting site for agate nodules to the east of the wash area off Graham Pass Road but it is hard to locate and may be completely worked out. However, you may try your luck in that direction as there may still be a few good specimens left.

28

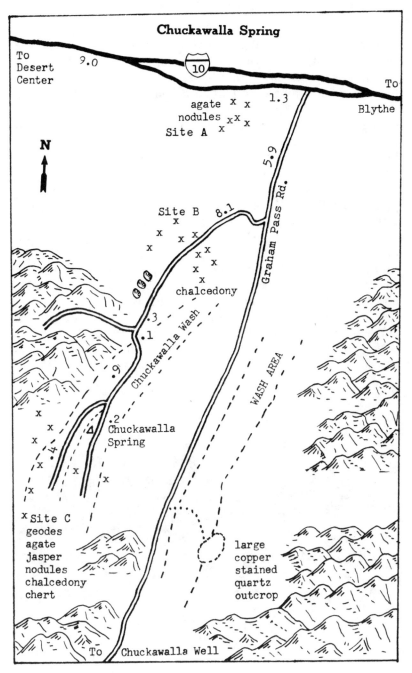

Chuckawalla Spring

To Desert Center

9.0

To Blythe

agate
nodules
Site A

1.3

5.9

Graham Pass Rd.

N

Site B

8.1

chalcedony

Chuckawalla Wash

WASH AREA

.3

.1

.9

.2

△ Chuckawalla Spring

Site C
geodes
agate
jasper
nodules
chalcedony
chert

large
copper
stained
quartz
outcrop

To Chuckawalla Well

BIG RIVER

These locations offer the collector a good selection of jasper and agate. The last two-tenths of a mile leading to the rainbow jasper site are washed out and most vehicles will not be able to make it all the way. Plan to hike a short distance from where you are forced to park. Much of the jasper found here is grainy and incapable of taking a polish. Some, however, is outstanding. There are lots of tan, orange, red and yellow materials, with a few pieces displaying beautiful swirls of color. The prize, however, is the rainbow variety consisting of vivid, multi-colored bands.

The westerly site is the more productive of the two, offering greater quantities. There, one can obtain agate, red jasper, mottled jasper and jasp-agate. The agate occurs in many colors and patterns, with the favorite being that displaying delicate fortification bands. The jasper here tends to be a little more colorful. The turn-off to this site is difficult to spot from the pavement and is just east of where the power lines cross. Simply head north at that point, and you will easily be able to spot the ruts a few yards away. The collecting site extends for quite a distance throughout the surrounding hills on both sides of the road, and, if you allow enough time and are willing to do some walking, this locale could provide a considerable quantity of outstanding cutting material.

The hill in the center of Site A

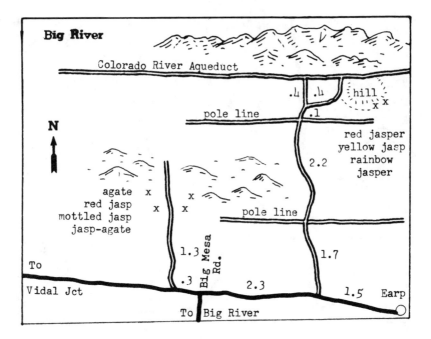

VIDAL JUNCTION

The large wash shown on the map has long been known for its chalcedony and, at one time, offered a good quantity of well-formed roses. Now, however, those roses are considerably more difficult to find. There are still lots of chunks suitable for tumbling and cutting, but the nice bubbly specimens are few and far between. It makes no difference where in the wash you search, though regions to the north do seem to be slightly more productive. Generally, the chalcedony can be found just about anywhere from Highway 95 extending east approximately one mile. More can be obtained near the mountains, about four and one-half miles farther along.

The best method for working this site is to simply park off the pavement and walk east through the wash. The bright white chalcedony is easy to spot against the darker soil and it doesn't take long to gather quite a few nice pieces.

31

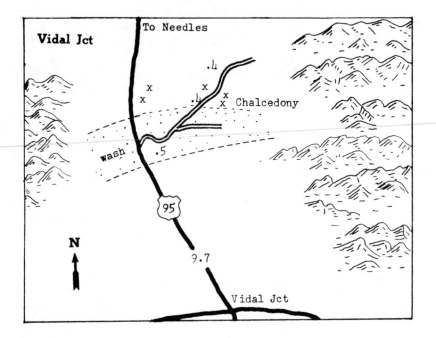

Chalcedony from Site A

TURTLE MOUNTAINS

The region surrounding the Turtle Mountains has long been known for its beautiful chalcedony roses and agate. Just about any spot you choose to stop at near the foothills may be a productive site.   Three proven locales are shown on the map. Site A is extensive, but it is necessary to do some hiking on either side of the road to find the best material. Site B was once very productive, but, over the years, a great deal has been removed. It is still worth the stop, however, since each rain seems to uncover some thing new. The best collecting is at Site C, but you must have four-wheel drive to get there. The road is very rough and even washed out in places. Because the trip is so difficult, though, there is still lots to be found there. Simply search the terrain sourrounding the "Mary's Canyon/Ruth's Canyon" sign, at the intersection illustrated on the map. It is suggested that at least two vehicles make the journey to Site C, in the event one should get stuck.

A selection of chalcedony from Site A

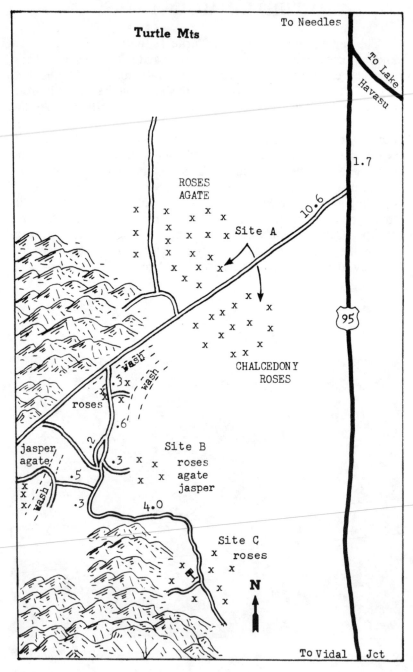

Turtle Mts

To Needles

To Lake
Havasu

1.7

ROSES
AGATE

x   x   x
    x   x
x   x   x   x   x Site A
    x   x   x
    x   x   x
    x   x   x
        x   x
            x

10.6

95

x
x   x   x
x   x   x   x
    x   x   x   x
        x   x   x
            x x

wash

CHALCEDONY
ROSES

.3 x
x
roses   x
.6

wash

.2

jasper,
agate

.3   x   x   roses
        x   x   agate
                jasper

Site B

.5

x
x
x/   .3   4.0

wash

Site C   roses
        x
    x   x   x
x
    x   x
        x

N

To Vidal   Jct

Preparing to collect at Turtle Mountain, Site B

LAKE HAVASU

This site features a little hill composed primarily of agate and jasper in a multitude of pattern and color combinations. In addition to the hill itself, much of the surrounding terrain contains more cutting material. Some of the specimens have a brown, blue, gray or white drusy quartz crust, making them very desirable for display as is. One could easily get carried away here, filling a vehicle in a short amount of time. There is lace agate, moss agate and a patchwork variety, consisting of virtually every color imaginable. In addition, one can obtain brecciated jasper, colorful opalite and lots of chalcedony. The quality varies greatly, so take time to find only the best. To get the largest pieces, it will most likely be necessary to attack the hill with a sledge hammer and gads. Simply start to work at any place you feel shows particularly good color and quality. There is so much available lying on the ground, however, that this extra work may not be necessary. Additional collecting can be done in the large wash to the south.

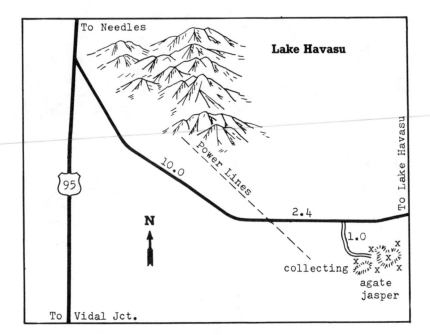

To Needles

Lake Havasu

95

Power Lines

10.0

2.4

To Lake Havasu

N

1.0

collecting

X X X
X X X
X X X

agate
jasper

To Vidal Jct.

Looking for specimens below jasper and agate hill

DANBY

Site A offers a good quantity of colorful translucent opalite. At the given mileage, you will be able to see the pits dug by previous rockhounds. Lots of small pieces can be picked up from the ground, especially near these pits, but the larger specimens are obtained by digging into the soft sand. The opalite occurs in a variety of colors, and some contain moss inclusions. Be sure to sample a number of different spots since the colors vary from pit to pit.

Site B, which is a small dump, can be seen from the road. There you will be able to find orpiment and realgar, the colorful orange and red ores of arsenic. Because of the arsenic content, however, it is imperative that you not get any into your mouth. On the dumps at Site C, there is fluorescent opalite, some of which contains metallic sphalerite. This is a private claim, but, at the time of publication, the owner allowed collectors onto the property if they did not enter or damage any of the buildings. Be sure to reconfirm this status before taking any mineral samples. Site D boasts malachite and chrysocolla, but most is very grainy and incapable of taking a polish. Some of the more sizeable pieces, however, are nice for display. While in the area, be sure to take time to inspect the washes. Nice agate, jasper, chalcedony, malachite and chrysocolla can often be found there, in random concentrations.

Collecting at Danby near Site A

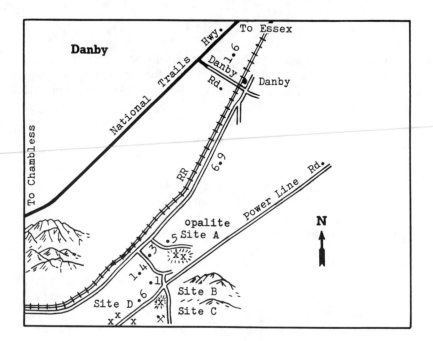

GOFFS

Slightly more than eleven miles north of Goffs is a most productive wash. Throughout it and among the hills and cliffs on both sides extending for at least one mile, you can find petrified reeds, palm and wood, as well as opalite, agate and jasper. If your vehicle can't travel in lose sand, park on the road one-tenth of a mile farther north and walk. Look in the wash for scattered amounts of material, and on the cliffs and banks for the deposits themselves. This is one of those locations where you can find quite a lot in a short amount of time. The opalite occurs in a variety of colors, and much contains excellent moss inclusions. The petrified reed is also very nice and offers many creative cutting possibilities. Be sure to take time to collect only the best.

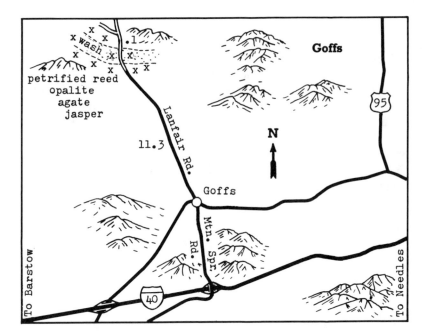

A sample of what can be found

CADIZ

From where you must park, at the base of the hill, there is a trail leading to the reddish-brown, trilobite-bearing shale. Choose what you feel is a promising spot and use a hammer and chisel to remove as big a chunk as possible. Then, carefully split it along one of the bedding planes with a sturdy knife; maybe you'll uncover a fossil. It takes patience and skill to expose complete specimens, but, with practice, you should develop the technique. If you continue along the trail to its end, you'll find an abandoned quarry that holds some colorful red marble, capable of taking an excellent polish.

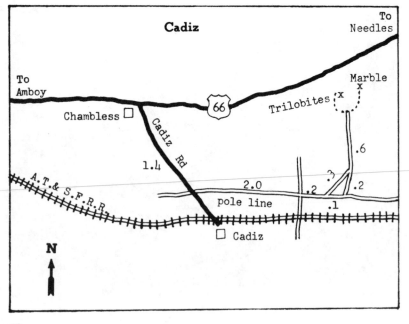

Looking for trilobites in the shale

A view of the collecting site

KEL-BAKER ROAD

The road to site A is filled with washouts, so drive carefully. Near the brown hill, you can dig for geodes and nodules, but only a few have crystal centers. Look on the flatlands surrounding the hill for chalcedony, especially across the ravine to the south. It is somewhat difficult to get to Site B. Use the map as a guide, following the faint tracks heading east toward the mountains, until you reach the desert pavement. Scattered over this pavement, you can find quite a number of chalcedony roses, but the concentration varies considerably from place to place. You must park and do some walking to find them. The sizes range from very small to a few that measure more than eight inches across.

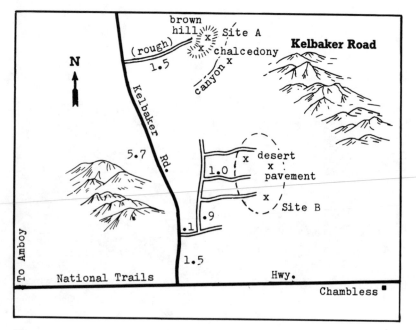

Parked next to the brown hill at Site A

The road to Site A

CHAMBLESS

There are many roads in this region, and not all are shown on the map. Pay attention to the mileage and there should be no major problem. The iron deposit is easily found due to shafts and the reddish-brown color. Look in and around the diggings for hematite and magnetite. In the washes, search for apple green epidote. Only a short distance farther east   is a deposit of limestone and marble in an abandoned quarry. Most of it takes a good polish and sizeable chunks can be obtained. You must walk a short distance to the quarry, however, since the road is severely washed out.

Some of the best collecting in this part of the Marble Mountains is in the next canyon. Here, among other things, is a tiny mountain of garnet. The dark red and brown crystals are massed together and small, but chunks of the crystal clusters are great for display. In addition, lots of green epidote is scattered about. Much of it contains bright metallic hematite blades, making it highly desirable to rockhounds. Farther east is yet another canyon and, at the given mileage, you will see a gray ridge of limestone. In it are many interesting fossils.

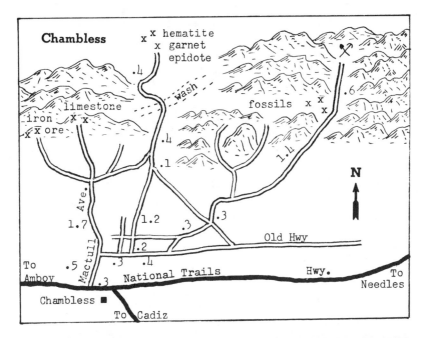

Chambless

x x hematite
x garnet
epidote

.4

wash

limestone

.6

iron x x
x x ore

fossils x x̄
x

.4

.1

1.4

Ave.

1.7

1.2

.3

.3

Old Hwy

.2

Mactull

.3 .4

N

To
Amboy

.5

.3

National Trails

Hwy.

To
Needles

Chambless ■

To Cadiz

Small mountain of dark red and brown garnet crystals

PROVIDENCE MOUNTAINS

The rocks and boulders on the dumps of the abandoned Vulcan Iron Mine are filled with pyrite and hematite. In addition, one can find epidote, limonite, magnetite and a host of colorful iron ores. You must have a sledge hammer in order to split suspect rocks and be willing to do some work. The pit is spectacular and worth seeing, but DO NOT go into it.

At the Bonanza King, look on the dumps for pyrite and galena. Also, above the main shaft, there is a fossil-bearing ledge of limestone. Be sure to visit nearby Mitchell Caverns State Park where you will be able to see some spectacular stalactite- and stalagmite-filled caves.

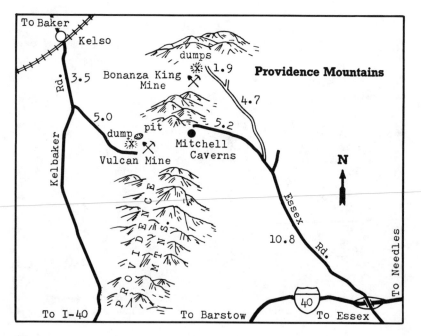

BROADWELL DRY LAKE

The final two-tenths of a mile leading to Site A is rough, and you may be forced to hike the final stretch. The road terminates at a large wash where one can find chalcedony and lots of top-quality agate, including beautiful flame and lace varieties. Pieces of common opal can also be obtained, in colors ranging from pink and white to prize violet. For those wanting to do ledge and gad work, there are a number of productive agate seams in the soft banks to the north.

Site D is only a short distance from Site A, but the road goes through a sandy wash for about one mile, making four-wheel drive essential. The tracks follow the wash around the mountain and then continue into a box canyon. From road's end search the foothills and washes for opal, green jasper, agate and chalcedony. This locale is not as productive as the others, but is still worth a visit.

The dumps at Site B contain copper ores, including malachite, cuprite, bornite and chrysocolla, as well as calcite and hematite. These mines have been abandoned for many years, but if they appear to have recently been reactivated do not trespass!

Site C is very difficult to find, since the road is severely washed out. In addition, one must travel many miles through soft sand. Because of these obstacles, four-wheel drive is highly recommended. Try to "hug" the mountains, especially as you approach the proper mileage. When at the collecting site search the hills and washes for colorful rainbow jasper, red jasper, chalcedony and sagenite.

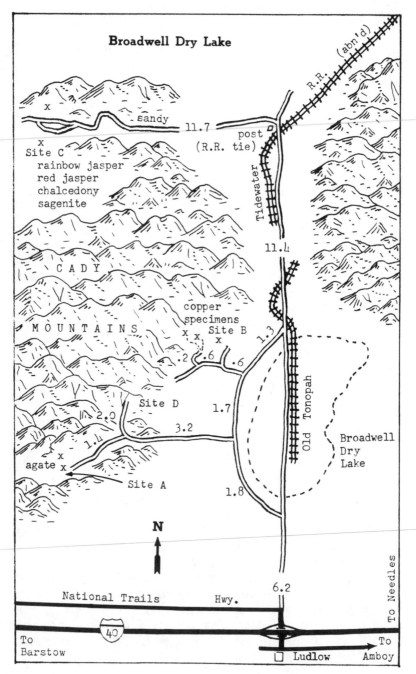

Broadwell Dry Lake

R.R. (abn'd)

sandy

x

x 11.7

Site C
rainbow jasper
red jasper
chalcedony
sagenite

post
(R.R. tie)

Tidewater

11.4

C A D Y

copper
specimens

M O U N T A I N S

x x Site B
x

.2 .6 .6

1.3

Site D

1.7

Old Tonopah

Broadwell
Dry
Lake

2.0

3.2

1.4

x
agate x

Site A

1.8

N

To Needles

National Trails   Hwy.   6.2

40

To
Barstow

To
Ludlow   Amboy

Site A

R.R. tie post at Jct.

Broadwell Lake area

CADY MOUNTAINS

Site A features a tiny hill just east of the road which is covered with an amazing variety of colorful jasper. Most have layers of brown and black, but one can also find jasper in shades of green, red and orange in an infinite variety of designs and color combinations.

Rhombohedral calcite crystals fill the cracks and cavities in the easily spotted contact zone, high on the hill at Site B. Be careful when climbing since the hill is steep and the soil is somewhat loose. Tiny bubbles of calcite can be found filling voids in rocks lying in the wash a short distance west of the hill.

Brilliant red, yellow and yellow-green hills mark Site C. The bright colors are due to the huge amounts of jasper lying on the surface. The hill farthest south seems to have the best quality and most vivid colors but all are remarkable. Take time to pick out only the most solid since much of the jasper found here is decomposing.

The road to Site D is sandy and rough so four-wheel drive is recommended. Travel to road's end, park and hike about one-fourth of a mile to where seams of rhombohedral calcite crystals can be seen running through the canyon walls. In addition, look for small chunks of chalcedony and agate in the wash leading to the calcite.

More jasper, chalcedony and very nice agate can be found throughout the hills at Site E, and the mine dumps at Site F affords interesting slag, which can be used to make unusual display pieces.

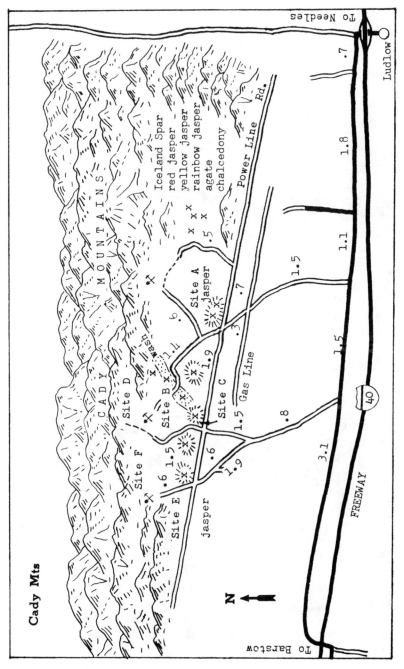

Cady Mts

CADY MOUNTAINS

Iceland Spar
red jasper
yellow jasper
rainbow jasper
agate
chalcedony

Power Line Rd.

Site A
jasper

x wash

Site D

Site B

Site C

Gas Line

Site F

Site E

jasper

N

To Barstow

To Needles

Ludlow

FREEWAY

40

.7

1.8

1.1

1.5

1.5

.7

.3

1.9

.6

.6 1.5

1.9

1.5

.8

3.1

1.4

.6

.5

x x x
x

51

Hills near Site A

The contact zone at Site B

HECTOR

The collecting extends throughout the hills illustrated on the accompanying map. This site has been known among rockhounds for years, and most of the surface material near the road has been taken. After each rain, though, it seems that something new is exposed. If you are willing to hike a distance your chances of finding worthwhile quantities of agate, jasper, jasp-agate, chalcedony and opal are greatly increased. It is not advisable to drive off the main roadway since most of the terrain on both sides is composed of very loose sand.

Using a sturdy rake to turn the soft soil is often productive, as it helps to uncover otherwise hidden stones. This is a site where patience is required, but, what can be found is of high quality, rewarding any collector who has the perserverance to spend some time here.

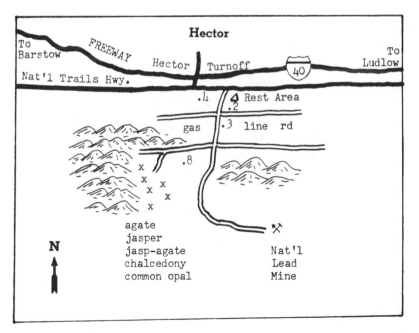

agate
jasper
jasp-agate
chalcedony
common opal

Nat'l
Lead
Mine

N

LAVIC JASPER

Many rockhounds feel that the jasper and jasp-agate from Site A is among the finest and most colorful to be found in the entire Mojave Desert. The main collecting area is only a short distance south of the Lavic railroad siding. Much of the prime material has already been removed since this location has been known for many years. There is still tons of very good material left, though, and it it well worth visiting.

The jasper and jasp-agate occur in an amazing variety of colors and combinations, primarily tending toward red hues, with blue and white quartz stringers running throughout. Such specimens, especially if they also contain areas of bright yellow and/or orange, make spectacular polished pieces. There is so much to be found at Lavic that you should take the time to carefully sort out all but the very best. Most of the material near the road is somewhat small but larger chunks can be found by doing a little walking.

At Site B, one can pick up more jasper but it is widely scattered and more difficult to find. The pieces tend to be a little larger, though, since this spot is not as well known as the other.

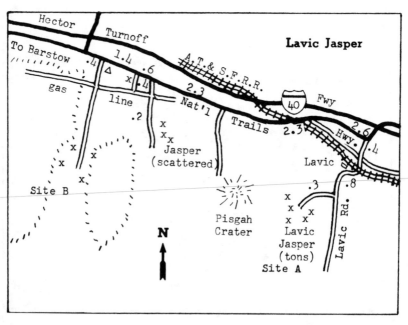

JASPER HILL

The road along the railroad tracks is sandy in places,   so be sure your vehicle can make the trip before starting out. Jasper Hill can easily be spotted due to its orange appearance. Simply park south of the tracks and walk around the larger hills to this most remarkable source of gem-quality cutting material. The jasper generally is found in shades of yellow and orange with black, brown, red and white stringers, some of which are extremely colorful.

As you hike keep an eye out for chalcedony and agate, as well as more jasper. The chalcedony occurs in many colors, including a prize blue variety. The agate also can be found displaying many different colors and patterns including clear, brown, black and red, some with nice moss inclusions. It is suggested that you carrry some water along since you must hike about one-half mile to the hill. It is also suggested that you do not visit during the scorching summer months.

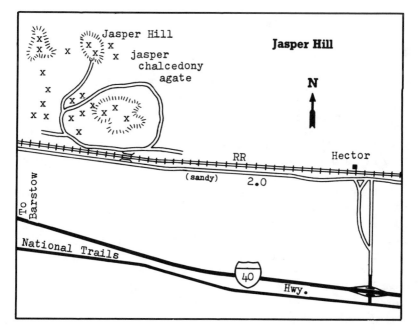

Jasper Hill

NEWBERRY

At this location not too long ago, collectors could gather hundreds of agate-filled nodules in only a few hours. Today, however, the little orbs are considerably more difficult to obtain. Over the years, the road to the site has been severely washed out, and most automobiles will not be able to proceed on the rough, unpaved road. Rugged trucks and four-wheel drive units can probably make it to the quarry or a little farther, but no matter what type vehicle you drive, plan to do some hiking.

The nodules and occasional geodes are found by digging into the crumbly white region above the wash, as shown in the accompanying photograph. A pick and shovel are needed to best work the deposit, as well as lots of patience and endurance. Most specimens tend to be quite small, but some can be found measuring more than five inches across. Many possess agate and/or crystal centers, but there are also quite a few duds. It takes hard work and time to gather a worthwhile quantity but the effort is usually well rewarded.

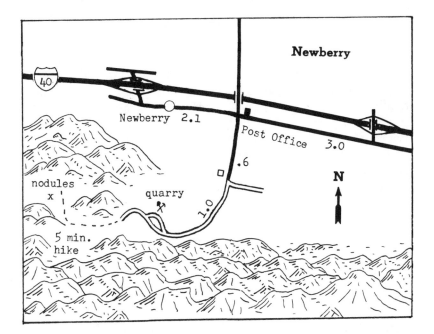

A view of the nodule collecting area

ORD MOUNTAINS

Just below the abandoned Grandview gold mine one can collect unusual orbicular rhyolite. It is found scattered all over the slopes and occurs in a wide range of colors and patterns. Be sure to allow enough time to find the best material, since some is quite porous and won't take a polish. Most of the "eyes" are perfectly round, with some measuring up to one-quarter of an inch in diameter. On some specimens, however, they are very distorted and produce fascinating display pieces. Be sure to also visit the Grandview mine for a spectacular view of the valley.

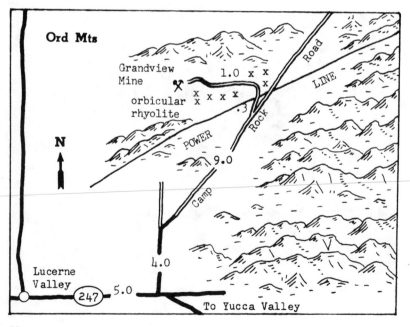

Samples of orbicular rhyolite

To Hun & Love 12-25-87

Orbicular Rhyolite →

Orbicular rhyolite scattered on slopes

59

STODDARD WELL

The Sidewinder Mountains, just a short distance north of Victorville, offer the rockhound some very colorful marble. Site A, the famous Verde Antique Marble Quarry, is probably the best known. The material coming from here is brilliant yellow-green and produces beautiful polished pieces. You must park at the base of the mountain and hike to the mine since the road up the hill is severely washed out. Site B is a much smaller quarry and it, too, has some of the yellow-green material, but the colors are not as bright as that from Site A. At Site C, one can obtain marble in a variety of colors, including pink, green, white, brown and black. Some chunks are composed of more than one hue, and they are especially nice when polished.

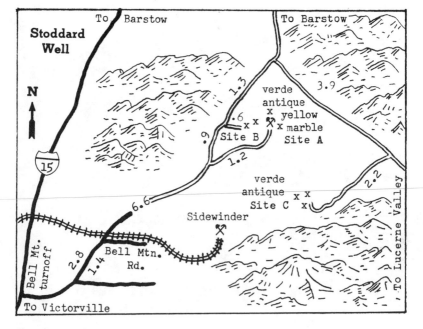

Verde Antique Marble Quarry

COYOTE DRY LAKE

Most of the onyx found on these dumps is solid white but some have bands of black and gray. It takes time to find the best but once you find a few chunks of the good material subsequent pieces are easier to find. In addition, some of the onyx contains cavities which are filled with beautiful calcite crystals. Collectors can also find small garnet and epidote crystals and chunks of the white onyx which contain the red garnets and green epidote make especially nice display pieces. The southern mine in this area is currently active and therefore closed to collecting.

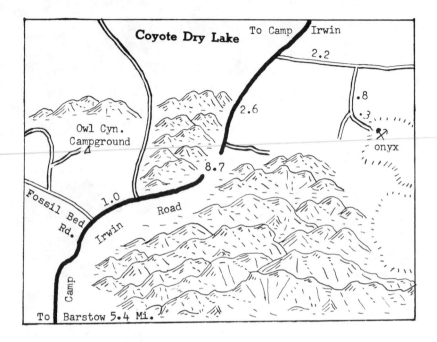

Coyote Dry Lake
To Camp Irwin
2.2
2.6
.8
.3
onyx
Owl Cyn.
Campground
8.7
Fossil Bed Rd.
1.0
Irwin Road
Camp
To Barstow 5.4 Mi.

Onyx

Area contains solid white onyx and some banded material

OPAL MOUNTAIN

Opal Mountain is just what the name implies, a mountain cris. crossed with seams of beautiful opal. There is some precious material to be found, but most are the common variety, occurring in a host of vivid colors, such as honey, green, orange, red, yellow and white. In the early 1900s, Scouts Cove produced precious opal, as well as some colorful cherry and range material. The best seams, however, were approximately 200 feet below the surface in very hard rock and, consequently, the operation was forced to close. If you wish to collect specimens for yourself, plan to do some work. Chisels, gads, sledge hammers and steady hands are essential to remove worthwhile chunks. In addition to the opal, one can find agate and jasper throughout the region.

Parked near the orange opal site

Opal Mt

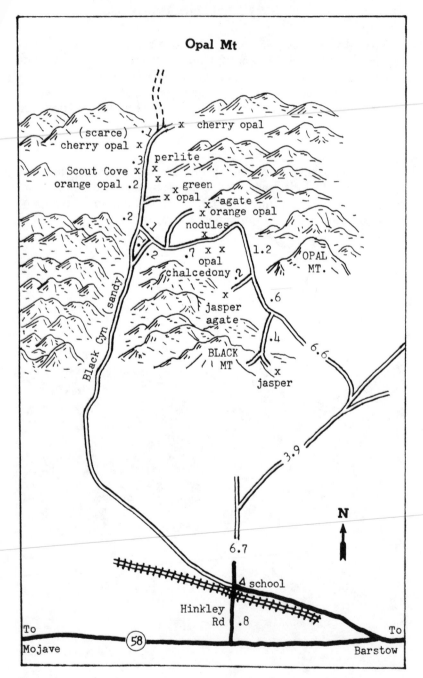

(scarce) cherry opal x

Scout Cove x
orange opal .2

x cherry opal

.1

.3 x perlite
x
x

x green
x opal

x agate
x orange opal
nodules
x

.2

.1

.2

.7 x x
opal
chalcedony .?

x

jasper
agate

x

1.2

.6

OPAL
MT.

.4

6.6

BLACK
MT

x
jasper

3.9

Black Cyn (sandy)

N

6.7

△ school

Hinkley
Rd .8

58

To
Mojave

To
Barstow

64

CALICO MOUNTAINS

The scenic Calico Mountains have long been a favorite location for rockhounds. Look for agate, sagenite and chalcedony on the cliffs at Site A. The chalcedony occurs in a variety of colors, and is found on boulders littering the hillside. Easily spotted excavations mark places where veins of agate and sagenite can be found. Site B features small amounts of chalcedony and jasper, with the most highly prized a beautiful golden-lace variety. Inspect both sides of the road, as well as the diggings to the north.

The abandoned dumps of the Pacific Coast Borax Company mark Site C. On them is a host of borax ores, including excellent colemanite and ulexite crystals. Dig into the soft dumps for best success. The last location, Site D, is noted for its agate and petrified palm. The deposit extends nearly one mile along both sides of the road so plan to spend some time. The wash next to the road is especially productive.

FIRST TRIP 1-24-88 ✷

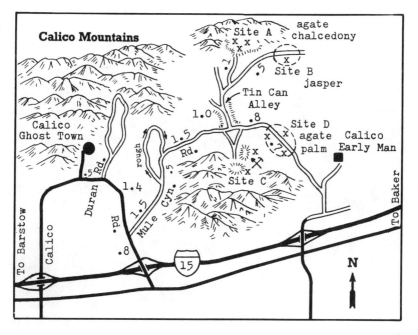

Parked below cliffs at Site A

Collecting at Site D

YERMO

A great deal of quality cutting material can be found in the hills and flatlands near the Calico Early Man Site, about 15 miles east of Barstow. Small amounts of agate and petrified palm can be gathered near the power lines and pole line road, as shown on the map, but the primary collecting is done in the hills northwest of the dump. Roam throughout those hills, looking for palm, jasper, chert and agate, in shades of white, brown and tan. The greenish colored hills seem to be more productive than the others, but worthwhile material can be found just about anywhere in the general area. Be sure to also visit the Calico Early Man Site, where you can see excavations of some of the most ancient known inhabitants of the region .

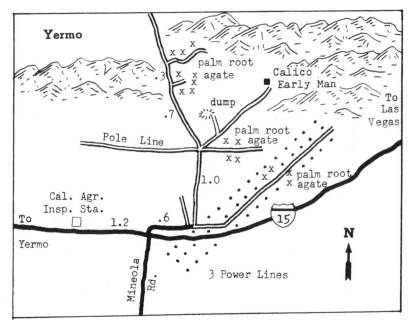

Nearly every rock on hill in background is gem material

AFTON CANYON

Afton Canyon offers one of the most scenic collecting locations in the entire desert. To get into the main canyon, however, it is necessary to ford the Mojave River. Most of the time this presents no problem since the river bed is composed of packed gravel and the water level is usually shallow. Occasionally, though, after heavy rains, the river cannot be crossed, so be sure to use good judgment. Allow plenty of time to adequately explore the entire area, since the best collecting is in the side canyons and upper hills. Look for flame, banded, lace and moss agate; brown, yellow, red, orange and bloodstone jasper; as well as opalite, in shades of green and yellow. Lots of bubbly chalcedony can be found, most of which is white, but some occurs in beautiful pink and purple hues. About halfway through the main canyon you will see a ledge composed of rhombohedral calcite crystals. They are fascinating and great for display in mineral collections.

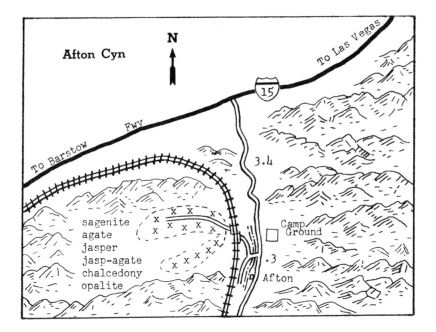

Site of main canyon and collecting area

ALVORD MOUNTAINS

The Alvord Gold Mine started operation in 1881 and prospered for many years. As costs increased, though, it was forced to shut down in the early 1900s. At the time of this writing, the Alvord is abandoned and collectors are able to find a wealth of nice mineral specimens on the dumps and in the washes throughout the area. One can obtain red, brown and yellow jasper, colorful agate and, in addition, some beautiful blue and white rhombohedral calcite crystals which cling to many of the boulders. On the dumps there is chrysocolla, malachite and even some hematite. A few years ago there was an attempt to reopen the Alvord, but it was not successful. However, if it appears the mine is in opera-tion, don't trespass.

Field Siding offers colorful agate, jasper, chert and an occasional piece of brown petrified wood The material is scattered through-out the area shown on the map, but regions near the road have been thoroughly picked over. It is still worth the stop, though, especially if you are willing to do some walking.

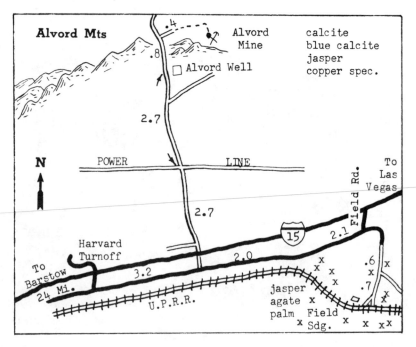

FIELD ROAD

These two collecting sites, on opposite sides of Interstate 15, offer the rockhound a good variety of cutting materials. Site A is extensive, extending south from the highway quite a distance past the railroad tracks. Scattered throughout this area one can find jasper and agate, as well as an occasional piece of petrified wood. Since it is not far from pavement, much of the material near the road has been taken, making it necessary to do a little hiking to find worthwhile quantities. Most specimens are small, but the nice colors and patterns help to make up for that deficiency.

Site B seems to have a little more available, even though, as at Site A, the pieces are generally small. Here you will be able to gather more jasper, agate and jasp-agate, in a wide variety of colors and patterns, as well as a rare piece of petrified wood. This site is also extensive, and, as was the case before, it is generally beneficial to hike away from the road in order to find larger pieces and better concentrations.

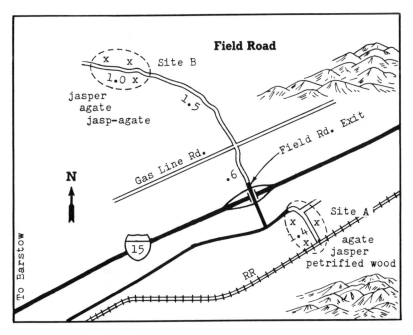

TOLTEC MINE

Both the Toltec Mine and the talc mine offer the collector some fine mineral specimens. At the talc mine, one can obtain brilliant white chunks of talc, some of which is covered with black, fern-like pyrolusite dendrites. The dendrites look like fossil ferns and make excellent display pieces. At the Toltec, you will find small, but beautifully colored turquoise chips throughout the dump. It is suggested that you park at the base of the trail, shown on the map, and hike the one-quarter of a mile to the mine rather than driving around the mountain on the faint, rough ruts. Take a hand trowel, small screen, a pair of tweezers and a bottle in which to place your turquoise. As you dig through the dumps, the tiny, bright blue chips will easily be spotted in the white soil, and patient work will produce quite a number of them in a short amount of time. Do not enter any of the shafts, since they are very unstable!

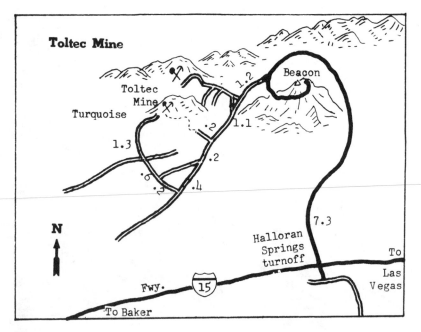

View from the base of the hill

KOKOWEEF CAVERNS

This is a most unique collecting site, featuring a series of underground caverns. Here it is possible to obtain cave onyx, in the form of stalactites and stalagmites, directly from the grotto walls and throughout the adjacent dumps. In addition, one can purchase choice specimens at the on-site rock shop. The beautifully patterned onyx is outstanding for display as is, or can be cut and polished to produce showy bookends, paper weights, clock faces, ash trays and any number of other items. Fees, at the time of publication, range from 50 cents a pound to one dollar, depending upon whether you remove it yourself or purchase material at the shop. There are camping facilities and pit toilets nearby.

The current owners are in the process of searching for a legendary underground river reputed to contain fabulous amounts of placer gold. The passage leading there, however, was sealed with dynamite over 50 years ago and no one has been able to find it since. The collecting status at Kokoweef changes from time to time, so, in order to avoid disappointment, it is suggested that you make camping and collecting arrangements before visiting. Current information is available by either calling (805) 482-4330 or writing to P.O. Box 1202, South Pasadena, CA 91030.

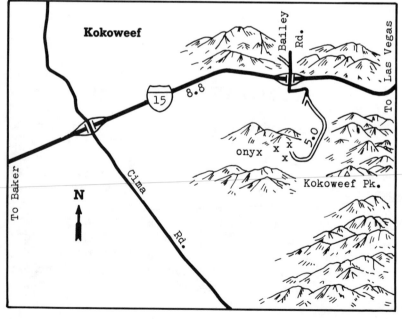

CLARK MOUNTAIN

At the time of publication, dumps at the Mohawk Mine are open to collecting, but those at the Copper World are CLOSED. Since this frequently changes, however, especially at the Copper World, be sure to confirm the status before your visit.

An abundance of minerals are available throughout the Mohawk dumps, the most notable being fine specimens of galena and sphalerite, as well as occasional pieces of smithsonite.

A number of years ago a large deposit of valuable royal blue azurite was discovered at the Copper World, and, shortly thereafter, the mine was reactivated. A considerable amount of excavation was done, but a few years ago the deposit appeared to be worked out and mining ceased, again opening the property to rockhounds. Shortly before publication, however, another group decided to try locating more of the azurite, and mining has resumed.

The Copper World is mentioned only because the collecting status does frequently change, and outstanding pieces of malachite, chrysocolla and azurite can be found there. Much of these brightly colored minerals are in the form of stringers shooting through a dark brown host rock.

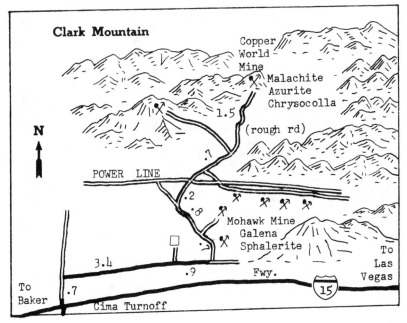

One of several mines in this area

Collecting at the Copper World dumps

TECOPA

Limited amounts of precious opal can be obtained in the mud hills across from the ruins of Zabriskie Station. Look for signs of where others have been digging. The opal occurs as tiny tubes inside the unusual clay concretions which are embedded in the mud hills. Most of these tubes are very thin, no more than an inch long and a fraction of an inch in diameter, and the opal only rarely shows fire. Be patient, though, since every now and then large fiery specimens are found.

There is another site about 24 miles up the road on Highway 127, which is extensive and offers agate and chalcedony roses. Simply park within the given mileage and hike or drive west from the highway. Scattered throughout this part of the desert is a variety of agate, the most prized being that with brilliant orange bands. The chalcedony roses are easy to spot, since their bright white color stands out vividly against the darker soil. Nothing at this site is particularly large or concentrated, however. It takes some patient walking away from the roads to find the best specimens.

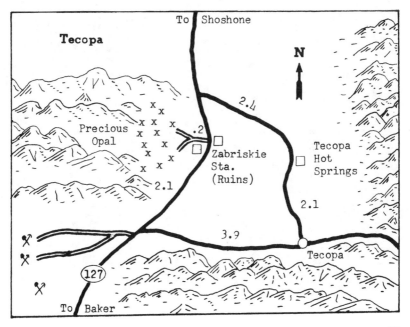

Close-up view of opal diggings

Adobe ruins across from mud hills

KINGSTON MOUNTAIN

Beautiful quartz crystals can be found throughout the portion of Kingston Mountain shown on the map. Most of the crystals are clear or milky, but some are prize amethyst varieties. Four-wheel drive is essential if you plan to drive very far into the collecting area, but the hike is not bad if you don't have access to such a vehicle. Look for single specimens throughout the wash leading toward the mountains and carefully inspect any boulders you encounter for cavities and seams. You will need a sturdy hammer and chisel to split the tough host rock, but your work will often be rewarded. Turning the soft sand in the wash with a garden rake will also be helpful for exposing otherwise hidden crystals.

There are veins throughout the mountains at the head of the wash, and, at one time, there was an amethyst claim there. Be patient and willing to do some work, and you will return home with many fine specimens.

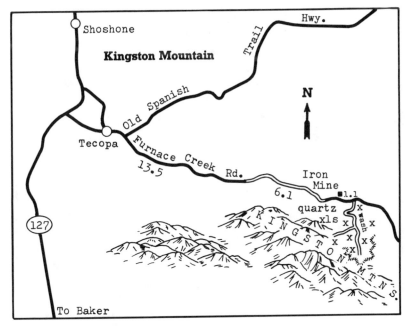

ACTON

The region surrounding Acton offers a number of collecting possibilities. At Site A search the hill to the north of Hubbard Road for small pieces of banded agate, massive olivine and colorful jasper. Small quantities can also be found in the lowlands. Site B is centered around the now abandoned Emma Copper Mine which can be seen from the pavement high on the hill. You must hike most of the way up since the old road is severely washed out. On the dumps are malachite, chrysolcolla and other copper ores, most of which, however, are no more than colorful stains on the native rock.

Site C is well known for its pegmatite minerals and numerous such outcrops can be seen throughout the area. Look along the road and in the surrounding hills at the given mileage for mica books, ilmenite and pink feldspar. The road to Site D is steep, but most rugged vehicles should have no problem. Look there for more mica and ilmenite, in addition to actinolite, green schist and hornblende. Pay particular attention to the large boulders on both sides of the road.

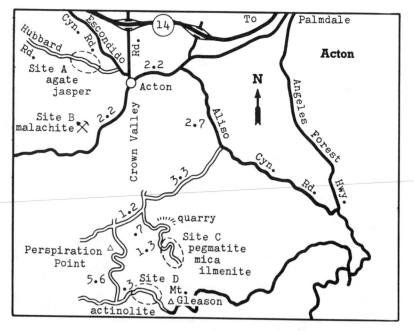

View from Emma Copper Mine, Site B

TICK CANYON

No active mining has taken place at the Tick Canyon borax mine since 1922. The property still is owned by the U.S. Borax Company, however, and advance written permission is required before collecting there. Simply write to J.M. Colvin, Jr., U.S. Borax, Land Department, 3075 Wilshire Boulevard, Los Angeles, CA 90010, and permission will be given, upon returning a hold harmless clause. On the dumps, the favorite collectable is howlite, but there also are other fine borax minerals available, including colemanite and ulexite. The colemanite is found in cavities throughout the many boulders on and near the dumps. The fibrous ulexite and cauli-flower-like nodules of howlite are obtained by digging into the soft dumps. On the hills overlooking the mine one can find jasper and agate. The jasper occurs in shades of red, green and brown, while the agate comes in a wide range of colors and patterns.

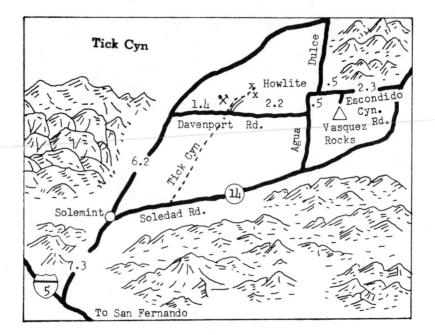

Tick Cyn

Dulce

Howlite
1.4   2.2   .5   2.3
Davenport Rd.   .5   Escondido
Cyn.
Vasquez Rd.
Rocks

6.2   Agua

Tick Cyn

14

Solemint   Soledad Rd.

7.3

5

To San Fernando

Parked just off the pavement at Tick Canyon

GEM HILL

Gem Hill is actually a series of adjacent knolls upon whose slopes one can find specimens of agate, jasper, rhyolite, common opal and petrified wood. Much of the rhyolite displays colorful bands, while the jasper and opal primarily are found in shades of green. The wood tends to be brown, with some regions of green and white. The most popular collectable at Gem Hill is the green moss and lace agate which can be found throughout the foothills. The surface material tends to be small, but more sizeable pieces can be obtained by digging into areas of green soil.

Allow enough time to also visit the old Tropico Mine and ghost town. A small fee is charged to enter, and the hours are 10 a.m. until 4:30 p.m., Thursday through Sunday.

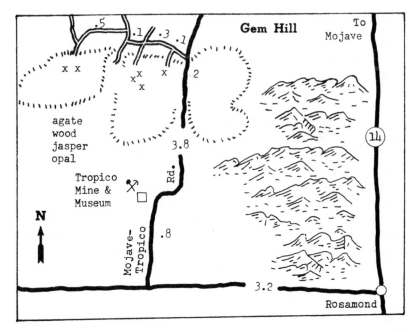

Tropico Mine and ghost town

BROWN BUTTE

Due to the proximity of this site to the Space Shuttle landing strip the road to Brown Butte has recently been closed to vehicle traffic at the railroad crossing. It is now necessary to hike from the tracks along the old road to the collecting site. The walk isn't bad, however, and the material which can be gathered helps to make up for the inconvenience. The most prolific spot is immediately west of Brown Butte, as shown in the photograph. There, one can find agate, jasper, jasp-agate and petrified reed, as well as an occasional piece of petrified wood. The deeply-colored chocolate brown jasper is especially desirable, and produces exquisite polished pieces.

Petrified reed is the prize at Brown Butte, featuring little "eyes" and tubes, depending upon which way it is cut. Fascinating pieces can be polished from this material, so have the patience to locate good solid speci-mens. Cutting perpendicular to the reed bundles produces the eyes, while parallel cutting unveils a series of lines.

There is a sufficient quantity of material on the surface to satisfy most collectors and each rain seems to expose more. If you have the energy, though, better and more sizeable chunks can usually be obtained by digging.

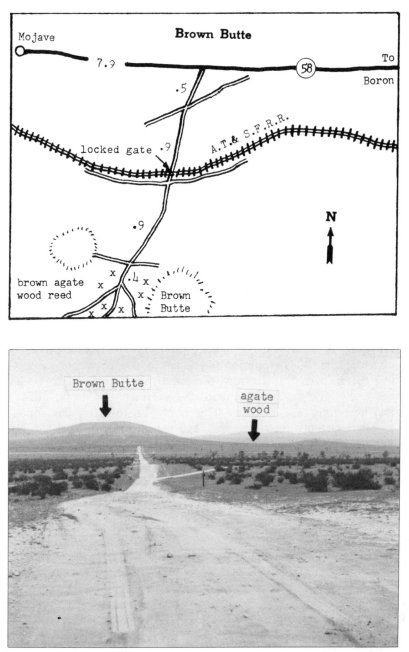

Brown Butte

Mojave

7.9

58   To Boron

.5

locked gate .9   A.T.& S.F.R.R.

.9

N

brown agate
wood reed

x
x   .4 x
x   Brown
x   x   Butte
x   x

Brown Butte

agate
wood

Agate and petrified wood can be found west of Brown Butte

KRAMER HILLS

The Kramer Hills, only a short distance southeast of Four Corners, have long afforded rockhounds many fine collecting possibilities. At Site A and Site B one can find agate and jasper as well as small quantities of petrified palm. The best known location, however, is Site C, the Kee Kay prospect. This is a privately owned claim, but permission is granted to anyone wishing to collect there. Mrs. Kay Burrow, the owner, simply asks that you let her know how much was collected, how many people were there and how long you worked. This is needed to fulfill her annual assessment work requirement. Send the information to 1004 San Domingo Drive, Santa Rosa, CA 95404. On the Kee Kay is green autunite, red, brown, moss and flower agate, and petrified palm. The material is found in float, as well as in veins. You can obtain small pieces of gem peridot in the black volcanic ridge east of the diggings, and the mounds between that ridge and the claim contain salmon dendritic opal and colorful agate.

Throughout the valley south of the Kee Kay is more agate, jasper, petrified palm and opalite, but it is not concentrated in any particular area. This is designated as Site D on the map. Our final location, Site E, is reached from Highway 395. In the wash at the given mileage one can obtain scant amounts of colorful chalcedony and agate. The prime spot, however, is on top, throughout the soft soil surrounding the sink hole. There you can gather beautiful jasper, agate and travertine onyx. Be sure to fully explore this entire region, since material can be found all over.

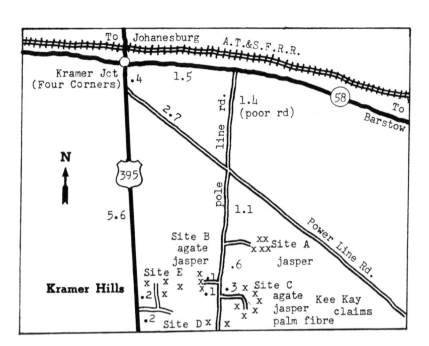

Most of the rock in the photo is agate, jasper and wood

CASTLE BUTTE

At Site A one can pick up chalcedony and agate which is scattered throughout the area near the given mileage. Both are somewhat scarce but a stop is frequently worthwhile, especially if it has recently rained. Site B offers more agate, as well as jasp-agate, opalite and an occasional piece of petrified wood. Most of the surface material is now gone, however, making it necessary to do some digging. The best wood is buried up to six feet deep but the labor is often rewarded with beautiful specimens. Look for places where others have dug as an indication of where to start. If you don't feel like digging, simply roam the hillsides. There is still some material to be found on the surface.

The easiest collecting in this region is at Castle Butte, Site C, where tons of agate and jasp-agate litter the hillsides. In addition one can find in smaller quantities, bloodstone, opalite, petrified wood land petrified palm. Take time to find the best pieces.

Many specimens litter the landscape

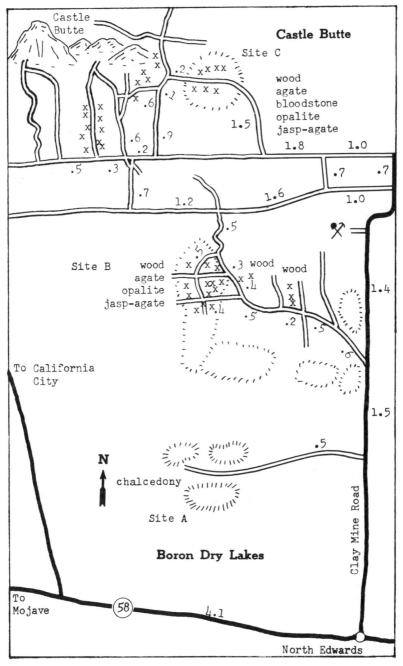

Castle Butte

Castle Butte

Site C

wood
agate
bloodstone
opalite
jasp-agate

Site B   wood
          agate
          opalite
          jasp-agate

wood   wood

To California
City

N

chalcedony

Site A

Boron Dry Lakes

To
Mojave   (58)

Clay Mine Road

North Edwards

BORON

The U.S. Borax open pit mine, near Boron, is one of the largest borax mines in the entire world. Collecting on the dumps is only allowed at 9 a.m. or 12 noon on Saturdays, Sundays and major holidays. Guards escort visitors to the dump area and return for them at noon and again at 4 p.m. It is not necessary to obtain permission in advance, just report to the main gate slightly before one of the designated times. You should wear gloves and have goggles, a rock pick, sledge hammer, chisel and gads. On the dumps, one can find outstanding specimens of ulexite, colemanite, kernite, howlite, bakerite and a variety of other borax ores. You will also be able to obtain excellent samples of realgar, orpiment, and calcite. Follow the instructions given by the guards and you should have a most productive collecting trip.

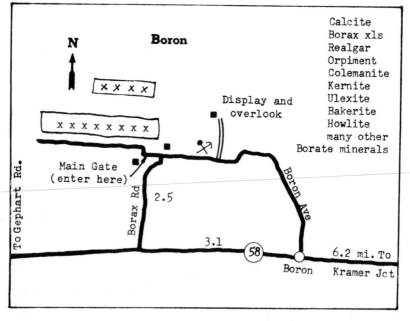

RANDSBURG

The hills near Red Mountain have long been known for their gold, silver and tungsten mines. Needless to say, all of those areas are protected claims and closed to rockhounds. Of interest to mineral collectors, however, is fuchsite, a rare, bright green variety of muscovite and yellow-green zoisite. Both can be found in and around the schist outcrop shown on the accompanying map. To gather specimens, break the schist with a sledge hammer and chisel, looking for telltale green areas. Be sure to check the other outcrops higher on the hill as well as any abandoned dumps in the area for additional minerals, including actinolite, epidote, quartz, talc, calcite and even some faint rhodonite. The fuchsite and zoisite crystals are the most prized, but the other minerals are also very nice.

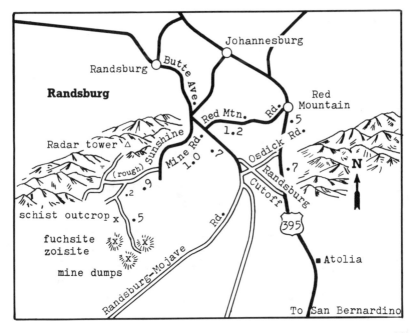

Schist outcrop, designating the collecting area

LAST CHANCE CANYON

The western portion of the El Paso Mountains offers rockhounds a number of collecting possibilities. Site A, the Nowak Mine, and Site B, the Barnett Mine, are both precious opal prospects. At the time of publication, a fee of $2 per person per day is charged to dig at the Nowak, and $1 per person per day at the Barnett. The Nowak is open seven days a week and the Barnett only on weekends. It takes lots of hard work to find opal, but it is there. Be sure to take hard rock equipment, including sledge hammers, gads, chisels, goggles and a pair of gloves.

At Site C, one can find limited amounts of jasp-agate, jasper, agate and petrified wood. Walk east from the road for the best concentrations. Lots of yellow and orange jasper, as well as more petrified wood can be found at Site D. The prizes here, however, are the tiny opalized twigs and rootlets.

Site E offers a spectacular view of Last Chance Canyon in addition to agate, petrified wood and opalite scattered on both sides of the road, especially the west. The wood and agate are generally found in shades of brown, gray, black and white.

The massive shafts of the Old Dutch Cleanser Mine mark Site F. Above and around these abandoned diggings, one can find petrified palm, opalized wood, black seam agate and jasper in shades of yellow, red and orange. In addition, you will have another spectacular view of Last Chance Canyon.

Site G is centered around a little hill covered with jasper and jasp-agate, in a rainbow of colors. Walk a distance from the hill for more jasper, as well as agate. At Site H, one can find more jasper, petrified wood and agate on both sides of the road, just before it starts down into Last Chance Canyon.

At Site I, one can find agate and colorful yellow and orange jasper near the road's end. To get to the prime site, however, it is necessary to hike up the creek bed, into the box canyon, about 100 yards. On the green hill, in the box canyon, dig for geodes, nodules and small crystal clusters. There are also agate seams on the ridge opposite the hill and more on the canyon floor. Look for elusive chunks of petrified wood.

Site J offers opalized wood, as well as more agate, jasper and petrified wood. This site is vast so don't be afraid to do some walking, especially into the large wash. At Site K there is more petrified wood, but it is necessary to dig for it. Start where others have dug before. Site L has scant amounts of petrified wood, agate chalcedony and jasper, especially if you are willing to hike into the canyon northeast of road's end.

The last location, Site M, is the most difficult to get to. Only go if you have four-wheel drive. The roads are steep and frequently washed out. Since it is so remote, however, there is still lots of petrified wood to be found. Look near the sandstone cliffs, which are reached by hiking about 100 yards along the trail from where you must park. Also inspect the canyon slopes below the sandstone.

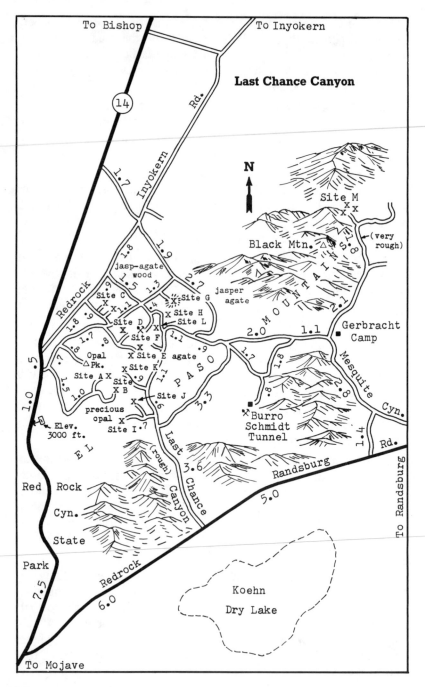

To Bishop · To Inyokern

Last Chance Canyon

14

Inyokern Rd.

1.7

N

Site M
X X
X

1.8

Black Mtn. △

(very rough)

1.8
1.9

Jasp-agate wood

2.7

jasper agate

2.1

Redrock

1.5
.9 1.1
1.3
.4

Site C
X
X

X Site G
X Site H
X Site L

Site D
X X X
Site F

2.0

1.1

Gerbracht Camp

1.8 .9

1.7 .8

.7 .8

Opal △ Pk.
Site A X
X
Site B

X Site E agate
X
Site K
.9

1.1

1.1

1.7

1.8

2.8

Mesquite Cyn.

P A S O

M O U N T A I N S

.5
1.0

Elev. 3000 ft.

precious opal X
Site I .7

X Site J

.6

3.3

X Burro Schmidt Tunnel

1.4

E L

(rough)

3.6

Randsburg

To Randsburg

Rd.

Red Rock

Cyn.

State

Park

7.5

Last Chance Canyon

5.0

Redrock

6.0

Koehn
Dry Lake

To Mojave

The Nowak Precious Opal Mine, Site A

Right fork goes to Site I and left to Site J

STEAM WELL

There are many crossroads in this area and travel can get confusing. It is helpful if you start at Steam Well and head first to Site A so you can sight on the obvious gray ridge in the northeast. A rugged vehicle is also essential since the road gets rough and sandy. In and around the mounds at Site A, stretching back to the main road, one can find agate. Do some digging in the mounds for larger chunks. Site B is the most prolific in this locale, and features a ridge of colorful opalite. The road is only a few feet from that ridge and opalite is scattered throughout the lower regions. In addition, agate and chert can be found on the other side of the road.

At Site C look on both sides of the road for more agate and chert. The collecting extends at least one-quarter of a mile in all directions. Blue agate is the most prized from Site C, especially that with moss inclusions. Site D is the least productive of the four, but still worth visiting if you have time. There are small amounts of opalite, chalcedony and agate throughout the region, and thin veins of agate in the foothills west of the road.

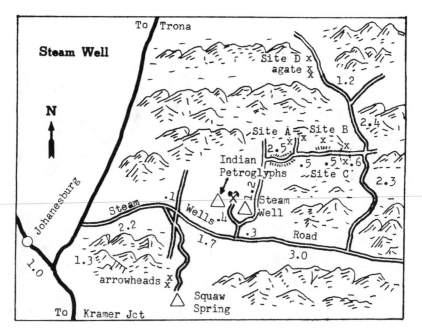

Parked at Site D

BEDROCK SPRING

This is a collecting site for those who like trips to remote and rugged areas. The road is very rough and, in addition, goes through lots of sand. You can only drive a short distance past the Bedrock Spring turnoff, even if you have four-wheel drive, since huge boulders block the way. From there it is necesary to hike. About one-half mile from the Bedrock Spring turnoff is a shallow canyon, on the left. At the far end you will see a tiny gray hill. This hill is covered with small chunks of very colorful agate and clear chalcedony. If you feel like carrying a shovel, digging into the soft soil might prove to be very productive. About one-half mile further down the main canyon is yet another side canyon and, at its end, there is a dark hill which contains more agate and jasper. It is not as productive as the first, however.

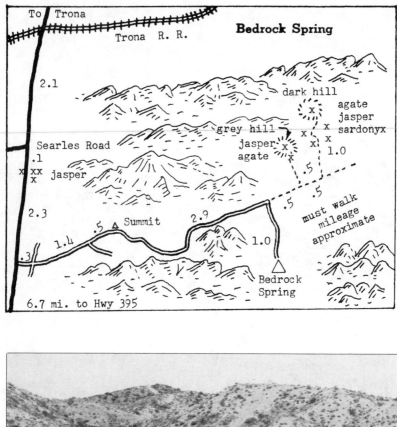

Bedrock Spring

To Trona

Trona R. R.

2.1

dark hill

agate
jasper
sardonyx

grey hill

jasper
agate

1.0

Searles Road

.1

x xx jasper
x

2.3

.5

Summit

2.9

1.0

must walk
mileage
approximate

.5

.5

1.4

.5

.3

Bedrock
Spring

6.7 mi. to Hwy 395

The agate- and chalcedony-covered gray hills in the first canyon

98

TRONA ONYX

Some of the most colorful onyx available anywhere in California can be found at Site A. This is the famous Onyx Mine, featuring banded and swirled onyx, in shades of green, brown, red, gold and white. Look on the dumps for loose chunks, or attack the deposit itself with sledge hammer, chisels and gads. At the time of publication, a fee of 35 cents per pound is charged for whatever you dig yourself and 50 cents per pound for onyx already removed. Campsites are available at a cost of one dollar, and there is running water on the property.

Site B is not overly productive, but does offer a few specimens of garnet in granite, honey onyx, white onyx, jasper and agate. The collecting is done thoroughout a vast region on both sides of Nadeau Road, starting at the highway and continuing about two miles north.

Site C is another fee location, the Aquarius Lace Onyx Mine. It is only open on weekends and holidays, from September 1 to July 1. The material, for the most part, occurs in tones of honey, brown and white, much of which display beautiful lace patterns.

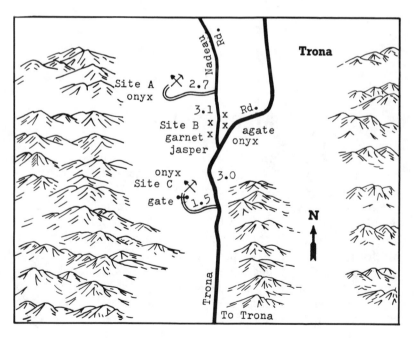

Trail leading to the collecting area at the Onyx Mine

SHEEP SPRINGS

The Sheep Springs collecting site offers moss-agate and moss-opalite, in remarkable quantities. In fact, a large portion of the hill, directly in front of where you must park, is covered with outstanding material which ranges in size from pebbles to large boulders. Most are white, with black dendrites, but some are pale blue, which are the most highly prized. Veins are found high on the hill for those wishing to extract material directly from its place in the mountain. Jasper and black agate are scattered throughout the lowlands, and small amounts of petrified wood have been found near the sandstone outcrops. Do not park or camp near the spring since it is a wildlife watering location.

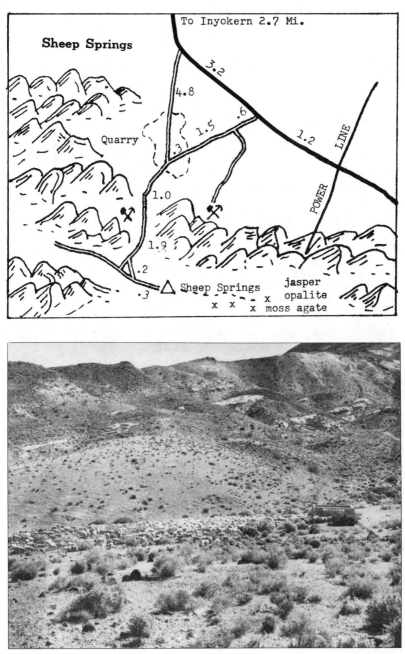

Sheep Springs map showing roads to Inyokern 2.7 Mi., Quarry, Power Line, and mineral locations (jasper, opalite, moss agate) with distance markers: 3.2, 4.8, 1.5, .6, 1.2, .3, 1.0, 1.9, .2, .3

Sheep Springs

RAINBOW RIDGE

Site A boasts tons of opalite, in veins and float. The colors include yellow, green, orange, pink and white, in a variety of patterns and combinations. Some of the material also contains moss inclusions. At Site B one can obtain more opalite, especially in and around the diggings on the hill.

To get to Site C, you must travel approximately four-tenths of a mile in a wash. Be sure your vehicle can make it before heading in. At the given mileage you will find lots of agate, featuring a spectacular swirled red and orange variety. Look throughout the area, especially in the diggings at the given mileage.

Site D is the famous Rainbow Ridge jasper location. This is a PRIVATE CLAIM, but written permission to collect will be granted if you simply write to the secretary of the Indian Wells Gem & Mineral Society, Inc., P.O. Box 1481, Ridgecrest, CA 93555. Rainbow Ridge features an entire hill composed primarily of jasper, in a remarkable variety of colors and patterns.

To get the best specimens from each of these localities, it is necessary to use hard rock equipment, including sledge hammers, gads and chisels.

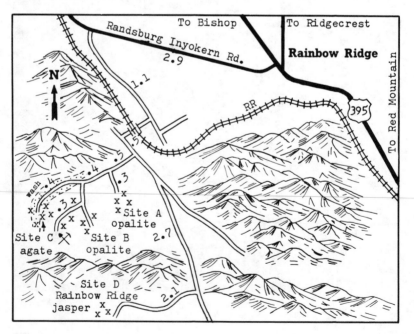

Rainbow Jasper

View of Site D, Rainbow Ridge

LONE PINE

Beautiful blue-green amazonite and an occasional beryl crystal can be found throughout the area shown on the map. This is not an exceptionally productive collecting location, since most of the specimens are quite small and strewn over a large area. The brilliant color of the amazonite helps, however, making even the smallest chips easy to spot. Look in the lower wash, as well as thoroughout the granite boulders surrounding the canyon at road's end. Also, if you have the energy, follow the main wash as it climbs the mountain. More amazonite will be found as you hike, and, on top, there is a spectacular view of Owens Valley. On the summit there are a few beryl and quartz crystals.

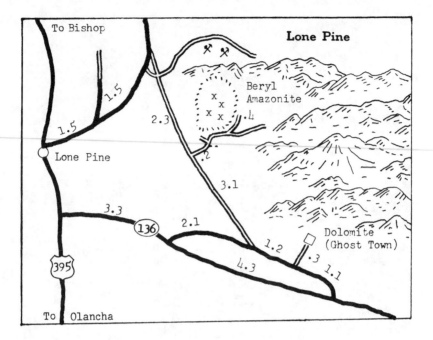

Parked next to amazonite- and beryl-bearing hills

BALLARAT

Ballarat has long been famous for its gold mines, but nowadays it is better known among rockhounds for its beautiful onyx. Site A is reached by traveling three and eight-tenths miles up a steep grade. Look for the rock slide on the right, about one-tenth of a mile past the old shack. Throughout this slide one can find tons of white and black onyx, as well as a good quantity of an exceptionally nice, orange-banded variety. There is a vein at the top of the slide for those wanting to try their hand at some hard rock excavation work.

More onyx can be found randomly scattered throughout the wash at Site B. This is the least productive of the three locations, but is still worth a short stop while in the area. The hills at Site C contain more but plan to do some diligent hiking if you want to find sizeable chunks. Be patient, though, and you will be rewarded.

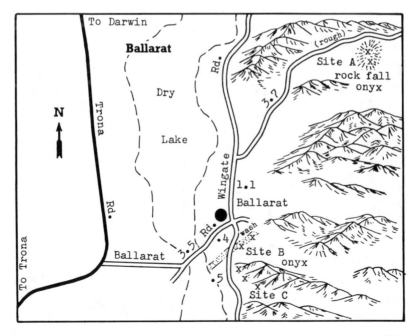

OWENS VALLEY

The quartz crystal seams extend about one-half mile along the hills to the east of the road, and are easily spotted because of the many excavations. A few crystals can be found in the loose soil below the diggings, but most are obtained by attacking the seams themselves. Use a sledge hammer, gads and chisels to break them down; maybe you'll expose a crystal-bearing cavity. It is hard work, but the rewards are often great.

As the road heads north toward the ruins of Aberdeen Station, it cuts through patches of unusual white soil. Throughout these areas are scattered countless tiny Apache tears. Most are very nice, occuring in shades of black, mahogany and brown. They are great for tumbling and some are even large enough to facet.

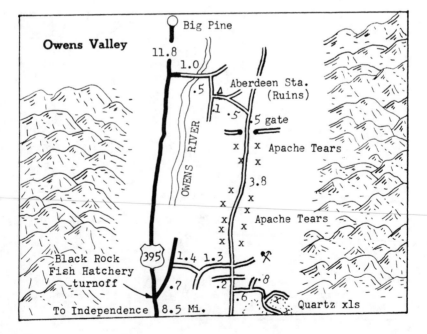

Quartz Xls

Seams of quartz run through the hills

BIG PINE

This is a great place to find smoky quartz crystals. They are generally well-colored and range in size from very small to many inches in length. Raking through the soil on the lower slopes will frequently expose loose crystals, but the most productive technique is to open cavities and seams found throughout the hill. You must have a pair of gloves, sledge hammer, gads, chisels and lots of energy, since this is very hard work. Find a promising location and proceed, trying not to damage any crystals that may be inside. Stuffing paper into the voids will sometimes help. Most of the cavities contain crystals. Plan to spend some time here.

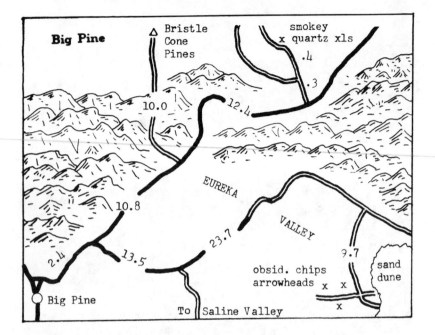

Smoky quartz can be found here

LOS OLIVOS

Most of the road cuts between points "A" land "B" on the accompanying map contain varying amounts of soapstone. The most prolific site, however, is Soapstone Hill, located about one mile east of the Figueroa Campground turnoff. This remarkable little knoll is easy to spot and the slopes are covered with specimens ranging in size from pebbles to colossal boulders. Much of what can be found in this region is flaky but there still is a remarkable amount of good solid material. That which displays little or no layering can be used for carving, while the other, if brightly colored, is nice for display. The hues range from gray to bright green but most is olive green. If you collect in the road cuts, park well off the thoroughfare and don't let any stones get on the pavement.

The road is paved but full of curves and is very narrow. In addition, there are many spots where trees overhang making it impossible for large motor homes and trailers to get through.

Soapstone Hill

Solid material can be found on slopes

109

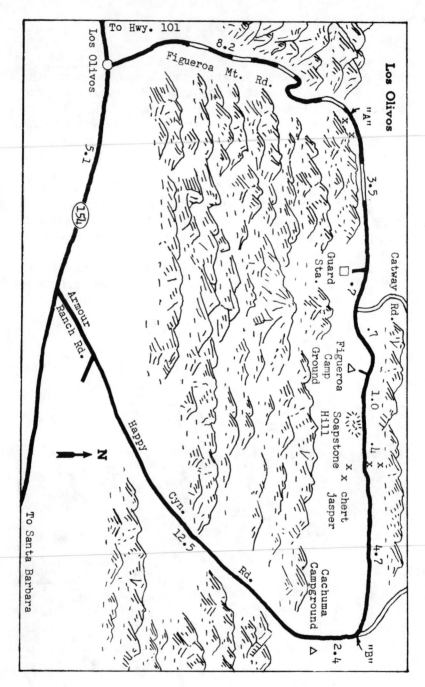

LAKE CACHUMA

Jasper, petrified wood and fossil shells can be found east of Lake Cachuma, in and around Ynez Creek. Park at the White Rock Picnic Area (east of the Paradise Camp Ground) and hike a few yards north to the primary collecting region. Search for the jasper and wood in the creek bed, on its banks and among the hills on the opposite side. The jasper occurs in brightly-colored shades of orange and yellow, while the scarce wood is primarily brown. The creek seldom contains much water and one can usually cross on the rocks without getting wet.

The shells are embedded in the easily spotted white limestone on the northern cliffs. To get the finest specimens, it is necessary to remove chunks of the limestone directly from the hillside using hard rock tools, such as sledge hammers, gads and chisels. The limestone is relatively soft, though, and the work is not too bad, especially if you are able to extract a few pieces which display well-formed fossils.

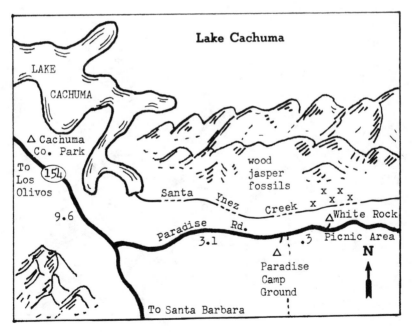

SAN LUIS OBISPO

The road leading to this collecting site is narrow and winding, not suitable for trailers. The journey does, however, take you through some extremely scenic areas, as well as affording a number of breathtaking views. The primary collecting is done directly below the relay station, as shown on the map, and boasts nice single and clustered quartz crystals.

At the given mileage, pull off the pavement and look carefully through any of the many rockslides. Some crystals will be loose, while others can be found filling pockets and cavities in the rocks and boulders. Pay particularly close attention to areas where there is orange soil since that seems to be a good indicator of a crystal's presence. You will need a sledge hammer to break up any suspicious rocks and a small rake is helpful for sifting through the rubble. Specimens measuring up to two inches in length have been found here, but most are very small.

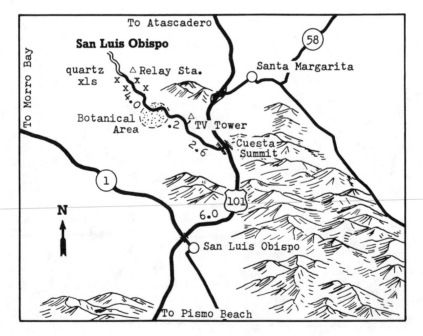

Relay station   above the collecting site

DEVIL'S DEN

Fossilized shells can be found in the road cut, on both sides of the pavement, at the mileage given in the accompanying map. It is imperative that you park well off the road while collecting here, since motorists will not be expecting to encounter a parked car in this area. To get the finest specimens, try to remove sizeable chunks of the fossil-bearing stone from the cliff. This is not too difficult if you have a sledge hammer, gads and a pry bar since the rock is relatively soft. You should then trim it so only complete and undamaged fossils appear on the surface. Such carefully-trimmed specimens make very nice display pieces. Do not knock any rocks onto the highway while working since they could create a hazardous condition.

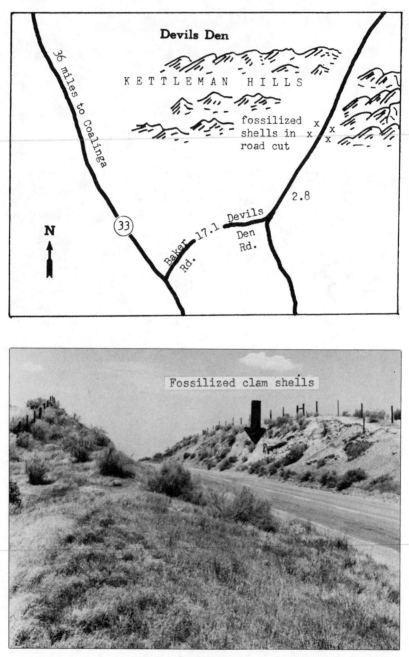

Look at road cuts on both sides of pavement

COALINGA

This site features petrified wood, chalcedony, chert, jasper and banded rhyolite. Collecting is done in and on the banks of a wash just off Highway 33. Material is found for quite a distance in either direction, but primarily to the west. The chert and jasper are generally quite colorful, and the rhyolite is a prize due to its delicate banding. The chalcedony and petrified wood are rare but worth looking for.

There are additional collecting areas just west of town along Jacolitos Creek where one can find jasper, coral, chalcedony, petrified wood, chert and fossil shells. These sites are all on private land, however, and currently closed to collectors. You may be able to get further information and gain permission to visit by inquiring in town.

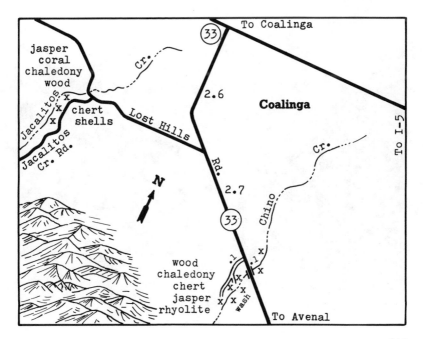

AGATE BEACH

Many beaches in northern California contain agate and jasper pebbles, but some are considerably more productive than others. One such location is Agate Beach, situated only a short distance north of San Francisco. To get to the parking area, follow the instructions on the accompanying map. From there, walk along the trail about 100 yards to the shore. The agate and jasper can be found throughout the gravel for quite a distance and are easy to spot. The clear agate with black spots is called oil agate and is highly prized by local collectors. The best time to hunt is as the tide is receding, thereby exposing a fresh deposit of gravel. Be sure to also look for abalone shell and petrified whale bone, neither of which is as prevalent as the agate and jasper but still worth looking for. This is a most scenic locale, and it doesn't take long to gather a good quantity of quality specimens. No digging is necessary.

Agate Beach near Bolinas

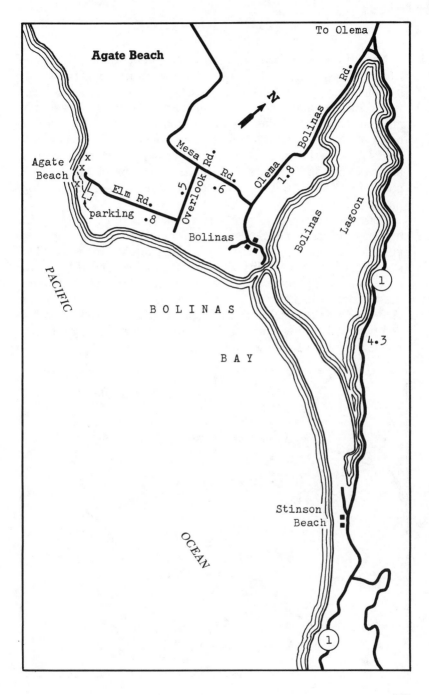

Agate Beach

To Olema

Agate Beach

Mesa Rd.

Overlook Rd.

Olema Bolinas Rd.

.5   .6   1.8

Elm Rd.

parking   .8

Bolinas

Bolinas

Lagoon

PACIFIC

BOLINAS

BAY

1

4.3

Stinson
Beach

OCEAN

1

N

COULTERVILLE

Beautiful green, mica-like mariposite can be found just west of Coulterville on Highway 132. It is necessary to use a sledge hammer, gads and chisels to extract the finest specimens. If you would like to obtain more and better pieces of this somewhat rare mineral, be sure to either visit the old Harrison Mine, about four miles south of Coulterville, or the Mariposite Quarry, five and four-tenths miles to the north. A fee is charged at the latter since it still is in operation, and permission to collect must be obtained before going in. Call Mr. Dolph Jacobs at (209) 532-4543 for more information.

Serpentine is found in nearly every road cut along Highway 49, between Mariposa and Coulterville. It ranges in quality from very good to very poor, with the finest being bright green and black stringers capable of taking a good polish. Be sure, if you have time, to inspect as many road cuts as you can. Once again, you will need a sledge hammer and some gads to remove larger chunks. Good specimens material can be found on the little hill about five and two-tenths miles north of the Merced River. Just look for the ruts leading west from the pavement.

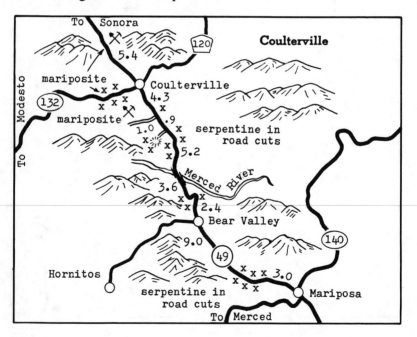

KELSEYVILLE

Good quality obsidian and sporadic pieces of colorful jasper can be picked up throughout the countryside just south of Kelseyville, especially at the two sites shown on the map. The obsidian is frequently difficult to spot since it can be disguised with a pitted, reddish-brown crust, but splitting any suspect stone with a rock pick makes identification easy. A good percentage of the obsidian is faceting grade, with the primary color being black. A few pieces of mahogany and swirled material also can be procured, as can occasional snowflake specimens. It isn't necessary to do any digging since so much can be found on the surface. Just walk through the brush, keeping a keen eye on the ground. There is lots of private land in the region, so don't cross fences to collect. If interested in exploring these areas, contact the owner beforehand.

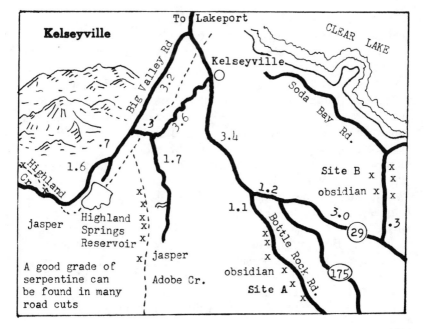

Collecting at Site A

JADE COVE

Nephrite jade and specimens of actinolite can be found in and below the beach cliffs, along a two mile stretch of coast in the southern part of Monterey County. There are crude trails leading to the various beaches shown on the map but the hike is steep and one must scrabble over some large boulders along the way. Be very careful and do not attempt anything you are not physically capable of doing. Most importantly, do not climb down the bank where there is no trail. The soil is unstable and can be very dangerous. The jade is found as pebbles and boulders in the cliffs themselves, as well as lying along the beach. Heavy digging equipment is not needed but a small hand rake and trowel are handy. Most of the jade is not translucent gem quality but there is a great deal of good green material which can be used for carvings or cabochons. Just be patient and willing to spend some time searching. Be sure to plan your visit at low tide when it is much easier to explore the entire stretch of beach. Don't get caught in an isolated cove when the tide is coming in. This could be very dangerous, and you could be trapped. Some stretches of beach become COMPLETELY covered with water at high tide.

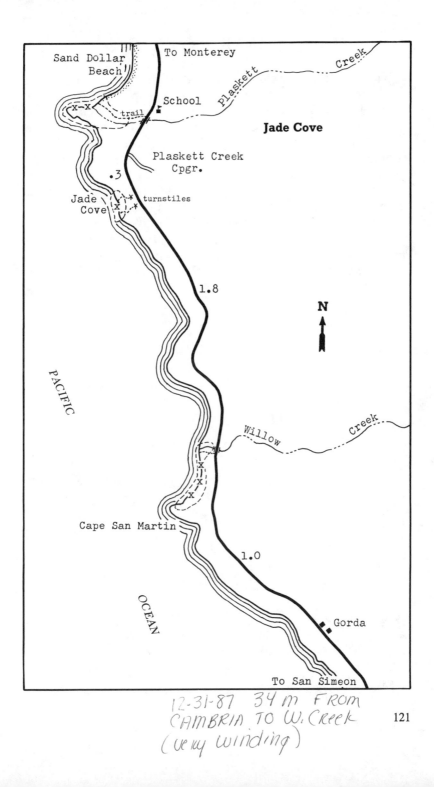

Sand Dollar
Beach

To Monterey

Plaskett

Creek

x–x

trail

School

Plaskett

Jade Cove

Plaskett Creek
Cpgr.

·3

Jade
Cove

x

turnstiles

1.8

PACIFIC

N

Willow

Creek

x
x
x

Cape San Martin

1.0

OCEAN

Gorda

To San Simeon

12-31-87 34 m FROM
CAMBRIA TO W. CREEK
(very winding)

121

BEAR RIVER

Nice pink feldspar can be gathered on the cliffs in and around the quarry shown on the accompanying map. The property is owned by Pacific Gas and Electric Company. Permission to visit should be obtained ahead of time by calling (209) 736-2576. Be very careful when doing any climbing, since much of the soil is quite loose. The crystals are most easily gathered by carefully examining the rubble in rockslides surrounding the quarry. A rock pick and small chisel will be helpful for removing crystals from large chunks of host rock. Small pyrite specimens can be found in the quarry, as well as along the river leading into the reservoir. Simply split any suspect stones in hopes of exposing a few of the golden cubic crystals. There is a forest service campground beyond the dam, if you wish to spend the night in the area.

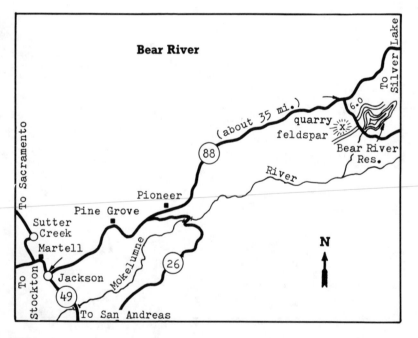

VALLEY SPRINGS

The area in and around Valley Springs is noted for its beautiful agate, jade, opal, jasper and serpentine. The most famous spot is the Snyder Ranch, just north of town, but that locality is only open to rockhounds one weekend in May. Similar material, however, can be found at the Hale Ranch, a short distance further south, and collecting is allowed there throughout the year if arrangements are made ahead of time. For more information, write Ed Hale, Box 207, Valley Springs, CA 95252. The fee, at the time of publication is $5 per person for anything under 30 pounds, plus 30 cents a pound for anything more. On the Hale property one can find, among other things, dendritic agate and jasper, colorful common opal and an occasional chunk of spectacular blue and red agate.

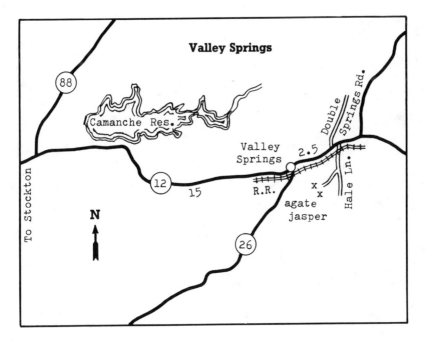

CLEAR LAKE

The hills and valleys just west of Clear Lake offer good quantities of beautiful and often flawless quartz crystals. These gems are unusual since they show no crystal faces and are extremely hard, making them highly desirable for faceting. Most are small, generally measuring less than one inch in length, but the quality more than makes up for what is lacking in size. They are primarily colorless, but some can be found in shades of purple, orange, smoke, blue or pink.

Much of the collecting area is on private land, so be sure to ASK PERMISSION before trespassing. The best time to visit is shortly after the fields have been plowed or following a good rain. Screening the soil in the dry creek beds often proves fruitful, as does gently turning the surface soil with a small hand rake. The most popular method of collecting here, however, is to simply walk through the brush looking for a flash caused by sunlight hitting the glass-like gemstones. Watch for rattlesnakes, especially during the warmer months.

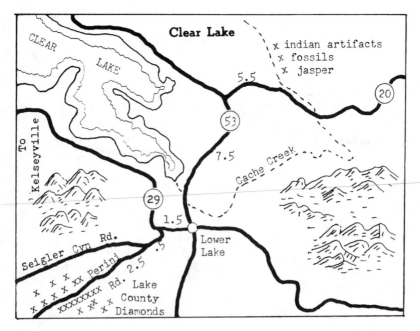

Collecting Lake County diamonds on Perini Road

View of collecting area along Perini Road

HEARST

There is a large bridge crossing the Eel River, which is shown on the upper right-hand corner of the map. It marks the center of this collecting site. Hike along the river and look for jade, banded rhyolite, actinolite and jasper. The mineral of prime interest is jade, in hues of white and green, some of which is of a quality good enough for use in carvings and cabochons. There also is a great deal of grainy, flaky and dark-toned material here so be sure to take sufficient time to look only for the finest. The jade can be found in sizes ranging from pebbles to large boulders, and it is sometimes worthwhile to inspect the larger pieces for areas of gem material. The jasper is red, yellow, orange and white, in a variety of combinations and patterns.

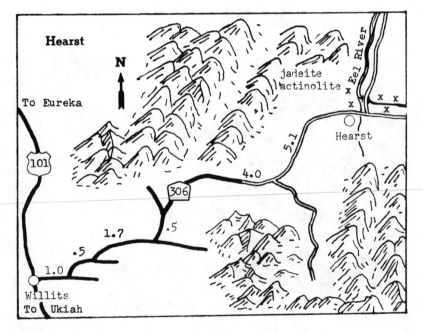

STONEY CREEK

The region surrounding the Black Butte Reservoir is noted for its colorful jasper and occasional chunks of agate and petrified wood. The shores south of Buckhorn Campground and at the head of Burris Creek are especially productive, as is much of the gravel and boulders lining Stoney Creek for many miles to the south. Carefully inspect all areas of erosion, especially at the above mentioned locations. Fall and early winter seem to be the best collecting times, since the water level is usually low, thereby exposing more of the bank. The jasper is found in a variety of colors and patterns, some of which is as fine as can be found anywhere. Yellow, orange, red and green are the predominant shades, with some containing showy inclusions of marcasite. Specimens range in size from pebbles to boulders, and a pick and shovel are handy for unearthing the latter.

The farther south along Stoney Creek you go, the more abraded the material becomes and, therefore, the more difficult it is to find. In addition, many portions of Stoney Creek are on private property, so it is essential that you first determine the collecting status of any spot you plan to explore.

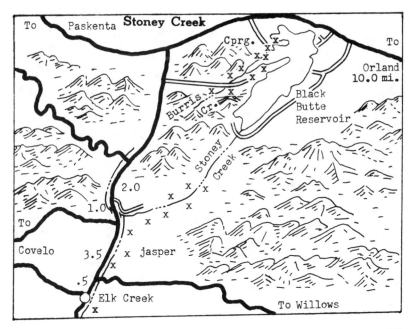

COVELO

The collecting is done along the Eel River, just west of the bridge, as illustrated on the map. Jade and jasper are the minerals of prime interest, with the jade being most prized. The jasper is brightly colored, in shades of red, rust, gold and brown, some with fine white stringers. It is generally of good quality and takes a high gloss polish. The jade ranges from dark green to white, most of which is mottled, and the quality varies greatly. Some are flaky and/or poorly colored, so be sure to take enough time to find only the best material. More can be found along nearby Williams Creek, a short distance to the west, but the best collecting is done on private property. Inquire in Covelo or at the Black Butte Store if you want more information about the site.

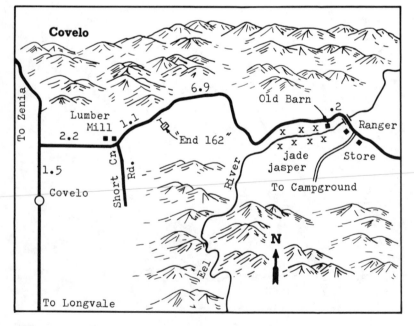

Collecting area near bridge

MINA

At Site A, search through the river gravel and boulders for jade and crocidolite. The crocidolite is a blue, fibrous variety of riebeckite, and larger specimens make excellent display pieces. The jade occurs in a wide range of qualities and colors, most being variegated in shades of white and green. Sizes vary from pebbles to boulders. Take time to walk a distance along the river to find the best specimens. This extra effort will very often be rewarded.

Site B is near the townsite of Mina, nothing of which is left. Look beside the road and throughout the trees and shrubs for chunks of maroon and purple chert, most of which will take a dull polish.

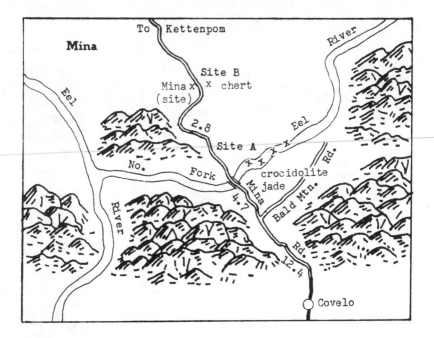

Map labels: Mina, To Kettenpom, River, Site B, Mina x (site), x chert, Eel, No. Fork, Site A, x x x x, Eel, crocidolite jade, Bald Mtn., Rd., River, Mina, Rd., 2.8, 4.7, 12.4, Covelo

Jade
Crocidolite (blue asbestos)

North Fork Eel River

KETTENPOM

Serpentine, jasper, chert and even a few chunks of jade can be found on both sides of the road at the location shown on the map. This site extends quite a distance throughout the brush and trees for at least one-half mile. Pay close attention to areas of erosion, especially the ditch on the east side. The quality varies considerably, but worthwhile quantities of gem material can be found with minimal effort. The serpentine is green, most of which is quite flaky. The chert and jasper are brownish-red and maroon, and generally occur in smaller sizes.

Excellent specimens can be obtained here if you have patience. It might be necessary to use a shovel for removing large, partially buried boulders, but, otherwise, most material is found on the surface. Do not do any digging in the road!

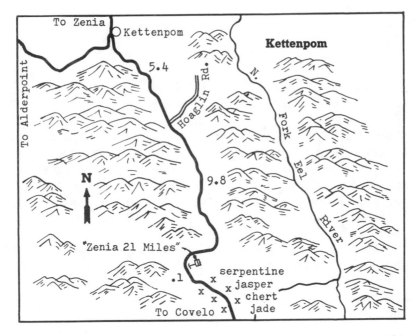

At the collecting site

ALDERPOINT

It easy to find this collecting site due to the large amount of green serpentine which can be seen beside the road as you reach the given mileage. Jasper, chert and serpentine are the minerals of interest here, and they can be found on both sides of the road for quite a distance. The serpentine is green and white, often containing tiny black inclusions. Some are grainy and/or flaky, though, so take time to find only the best. Jasper and chert are primarily chocolate brown, but orange specimens also can be found scattered about. Some of the jasper has contrasting white and black streaks which help make it very desirable for use in cabochons.

Don't hesitate to do some walking since it seems that the finest material is usually a distance form the road, partially hidden by shrubbery. Be sure to take a rock pick with you as you hike, splitting any suspect stones to ascertain their true identity and quality.

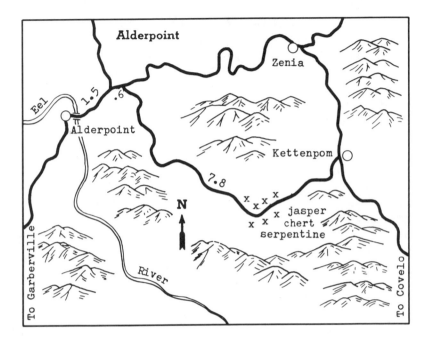

Green serpentine boulder

MOUNT SHASTA

This is certainly one of the most scenic rockhounding areas in California, located in the shadow of spectacular Mt. Shasta. The collecting is done in and around the dumps of an old copper mine, where one can find metallic chalcocite and chalcopyrite, as well as colorful malachite and chrysocolla. The prospect is difficult to spot from the main road, but, as you turn onto the ruts leading into the collecting area, the dumps can be seen through the trees. The green and blue malachite and chrysocolla are easily to find due to their bright colors, but it is necessary to split suspect rocks in order to locate the elusive chalcocite and chalcopyrite. Most of the malachite and chrysocolla are too porous and thin to polish but they can be used to make nice display pieces. Do some digging in the soft soil of the dump to find the best specimens.

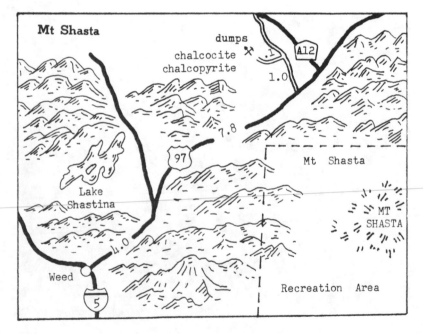

The dumps at the collecting site

WILLOW CREEK

At the given mileage, there is a turnout where cars can be parked off the pavement. From there, it is easy to spot the trail leading down the bank to Willow Creek. Look amongst the gravel and boulders, on both sides of the stream, to find fine pieces of serpentine and omphacite. The serpentine is primarily green, with tiny black and white specks running throughout, while the less prevalent omphacite is generally a lighter shade of green and more granular.

Be sure to walk a distance through the trees and brush and don't hesitate to split any suspect stones to help in identification. Much of the serpentine takes a polish, but the omphacite, at best, only produces a dull luster. It is nice, however, for display in mineral collections.

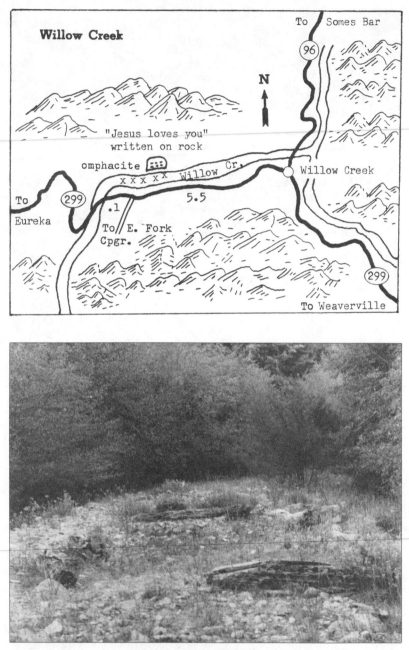

The collecting area next to Willow Creek

HAYFORK

Fossilized clams can be found throughout the cliffs behind the old Blanchard School. Simply follow the dim trail which leads from the school to the main collecting area. It is not difficult to remove chunks of fossil-filled rock directly from the hill with a sledge hammer and chisel, but, if you don't feel like engaging in such work, lots of fine specimens can be gathered by digging through the rubble down below.

The travertine is obtained by hiking east along the East Fork Divide Trail about four miles from where it intersects the pavement, as shown on the map. The material is good but the deposit is difficult to find in a somewhat remote location and you must carry out everything you want to keep. These factors make this a challenging, but minimally rewarding, location.

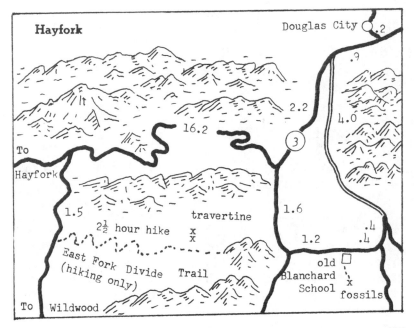

Fossilized clams

Looking for fossils in rubble below cliffs

ETNA

To get onto the correct road from Etna simply follow the signs toward Sawyers Bar. The deposit is easy to spot, being just off the pavement, and the marble is primarily white. Some, however, is light pink and/or green, with the most prized being that which shows all three hues. Good specimens can be found by carefully searching through the loose rocks or by directly attacking the outcrop itself with gads and chisels or a sledge hammer. Be careful when climbing since much of the rock is loose. Be certain you do not let stones fall onto the pavement, since that will create a dangerous situation for automobile traffic.

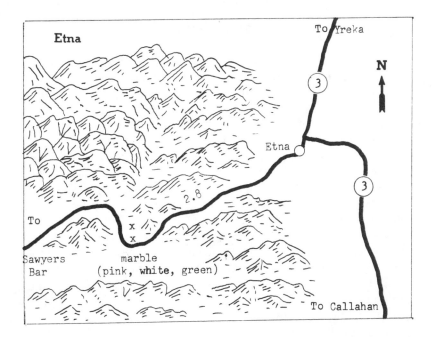

Marble chunks in loose rock

JENNEY CREEK

Jasper, rhodonite, carnelian, agate and petrified wood all can be found along Jenney Creek, just north of the Iron Gate Reservoir. Collecting starts where the creek passes near the Wilkes Expedition Memorial and continues for at least one and one-half miles. Search on both sides of the road, paying particularly close attention to the stream bed, the soft soil on its banks and any other areas of erosion. You should also examine roadbeds and berms, especially if freshly graded. It is easy to spot the gemstones, since their bright colors stand out vividly against the darker soil.

None of the collectables are overly plentiful, but jasper is the most frequently encountered. It is of high quality and comes in a variety of colors, including red, yellow, rust and orange. The agate is generally found in darker shades, with some containing interesting inclusions. Occasional chunks of orange carnelian can be acquired, but these are rare. The rhodonite is also scarce and difficult to spot, since it is usually covered with a black crust. Use a rock pick to split any such stones in hopes of exposing a prize pink center. Brown and tan petrified wood can sometimes be picked up, but it is not plentiful.

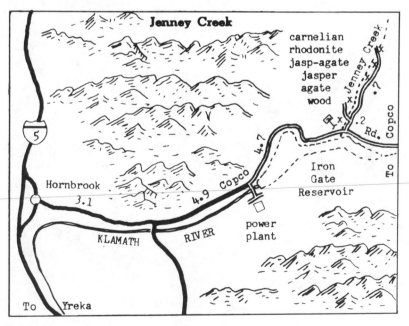

Jenney Creek, north of reservoir

SLATER BUTTE

Lots of good quality serpentine and occasional pieces of jade can be found in the abandoned quarry located at the top of the map. Simply dig through the dumps and rubble to find specimens ranging in size from tiny chips and pebbles to large boulders. Most of the serpentine will take a good polish and is dark green with random black and white areas. The jade, for the most part, is not of high quality, being somewhat pale, but a few worthwhile pieces can be found with patience. The collecting status of old mines changes from time to time, so if there are any indications that the quarry has been reactivated be sure to inquire about current status before digging.

Jade and serpentine can also be found at the lower site, but are more difficult to find since you must search through the brush and trees on the hill overlooking the road. The material, however, tends to be less fractured and, therefore, of better quality. Park well off the road, be careful when climbing and don't let any rocks fall onto the pavement.

Jade and good quality serpentine can be found in dumps

HAPPY CAMP

Most of the streams and rivers near Happy Camp contain boulders of serpentine and jade, some being of extremely high quality. In addition, a fine grade of rhodonite can be found, as can bowenite nodules and crystals of idocrase, garnet and pyrite. Probably the best collecting area is Site A, a private jade claim owned by the Indian Creek Rock Shop. At the time of publication, no fee was charged and the claim was being maintained strictly for rockhound use. It would be a good idea to stop by the shop to confirm that status and to view specimens of minerals which can be found there.

The rhodonite is difficult to find since it is usually covered with a black crust. Because of that, split any suspect black, blocky stones, which may expose beautiful pink interiors.

Near the jade claim there is a log blocking the road, as shown on the map. DO NOT drive any further, since, from that point, the road turns into a foot trail, and drops steeply to the river.

Site B, on the west branch of Indian Creek, offers similar material in smaller amounts. Ideas for additional collecting sites in the region can be obtained at any of the rock shops in the area.

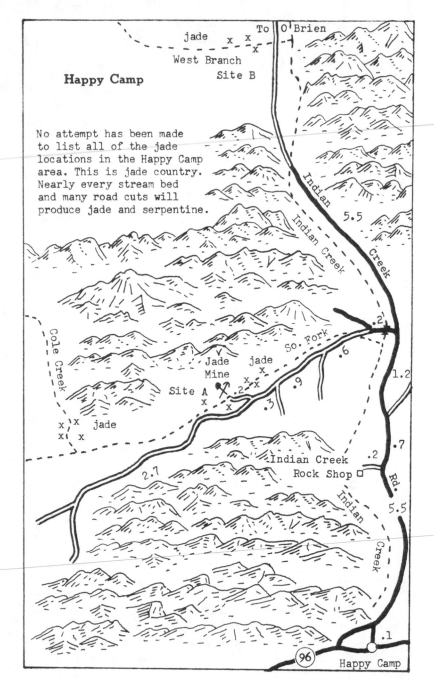

Happy Camp

jade x x To O'Brien

West Branch
Site B

No attempt has been made
to list all of the jade
locations in the Happy Camp
area. This is jade country.
Nearly every stream bed
and many road cuts will
produce jade and serpentine.

Indian Creek

Indian Creek

5.5

Cole Creek

So. Fork

.2

Jade
Mine   jade
x

Site A x x .2 x x   .6

x   .9

x   .3

x x jade
x x

1.2

2.7

Indian Creek
Rock Shop ☐

.2   .7

Indian Creek

Rd.

5.5

.1

96 Happy Camp

Jade boulders in stream

Examining a jade boulder near mine

PATRICK'S POINT

The beaches of northern California are noted for the agate pebbles which can be found throughout their sands. Some locations, however, are far more productive than others. One of the most prolific is Agate Beach, at Patrick's Point State Park, about 30 miles north of Eureka. To get there, follow the signs to the steep, but well-maintained trail leading down to the shore.

It is best to hunt shortly after the high tide has receded, since the beach will then be covered with a fresh deposit of agate-bearing gravel. Be sure to take a small collecting bag and pay close attention to the tides. Don't get caught in areas where you might be stranded if the tide comes in rapidly. The Park has a few restrictions as to how much agate you can take, so be sure to ask rangers about current regulations before collecting.

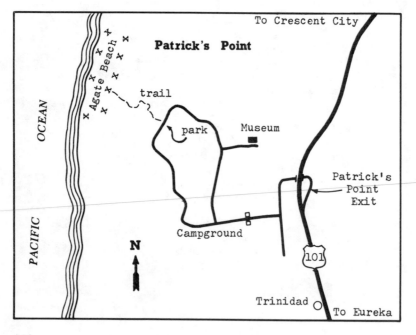

Agate Beach at Patrick's Point

PULGA

Beautiful apple-green vesuvianite and serpentine can be found in this most scenic locality. The road cut at Site A boasts lots of fine green serpentine, but, as you collect there, be careful not to allow any rocks to slide onto the pavement. This is a narrow road, and, in order not to block traffic, it might be necessary to park a short distance from the collecting site and walk back.

To get to Site B, continue along Pulga Road to where it intersects Camp Creek Road. Nice serpentine and occasional pieces of vesuvianite (idocrase) bearing rock can be found in the stream, just below the bridge. The best vesuvianite is translucent and looks much like fine jade. It is hard, and will take a very good polish.

In fact, it is so similar in appearance to jade, that it is locally called Pulga Jade. Continue up Camp Creek Road to the digging area, about nine-tenths of a mile from the intersection. This road is frequently washed out, but sometimes passable with four-wheel drive. The walk isn't bad, though, and takes about one-half hour. Search for the vesuvianite and serpentine in the rubble below the diggings or attack the rock with sledge hammer, gads and pry bars. The gem vesuvianite occurs as small nodules and lenses in the host rock and is relatively easy to spot. It takes a lot of work to extract large quantities, however, but whatever you are able to find will be well worth the effort.

Site C is located behind a highway maintenance station and is reached by hiking up a steep trail past an Indian burial ground. There is a road, about one-tenth of a mile east of the maintenance yard, which intersects that trail. Park across the highway and walk from there. The vesuvianite and serpentine are found in a manner similar to Site B. Be sure to also spend some time looking through the gravel and boulders lining Mill Creek for additional specimens.

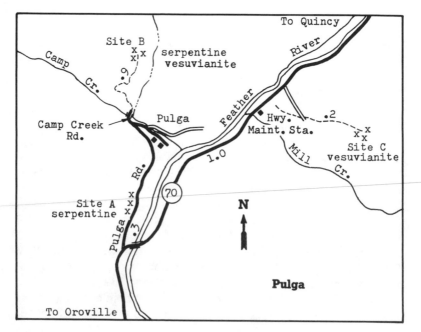

SUSANVILLE

Turn from Highway 139 at the Jacks Valley Monument, as shown on the map, to get to Site A. From the moment you leave the pavement, continue at least one mile to a site where it is possible to find agate, jasper and petrified wood scattered on both sides of the road. Pay particularly close attention to areas of erosion, especially along the banks of the creek to the south. Most of the wood is brown and has been slightly abraded by the river. The chunks of jasper come in shades of orange, brown and black and are generally small. The agate is gray and black, but, if contrast is good, it can be used to make exquisite polished pieces. Concentrations vary greatly, so, if you don't find much at one spot, simply move a little further along and try again.

Site B is reached by parking to the side of the road and walking about 100 yards down the hill to Willard Creek. This location offers more agate, jasper and petrified wood, as well as occasional chunks of green serpentine and Apache tears. Much of this material is difficult to spot, since it has been rounded and abraded by the river. Therefore, any suspect stones should be split to determine their true identity. The wood tends to be a little lighter in color here, tan or ash-white. Most of the agate is clear or gray, but there also is a red and green variety available which is a real prize.

Willard Creek, Site B

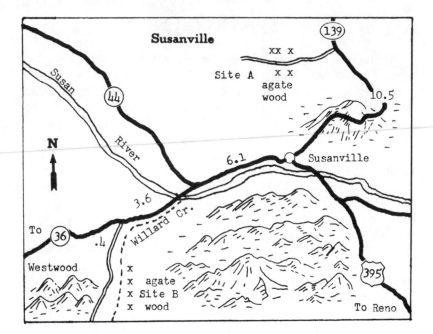

ADIN

Chunks of banded rhyolite can be found a short distance west of the abandoned town of Hayden Hill, as shown on the map. The rhyolite ranges in size from little chips to good-sized boulders, and the quality also varies considerably. Some is fairly plain, while other is filled with bands, swirls and splotches, in vividly contrasting shades of brown and rust. Walk through the hills and split any pieces you may come upon to help ascertain their quality. Most will take a dull polish and can be used to make outstanding clock faces, bookends and larger cabochons.

Do not venture into any of the old buildings or mine shafts at Hayden Hill, since they are very unstable. You may, however, be able to find some nice mineral specimens on the dumps of this once prosperous gold and silver mine.

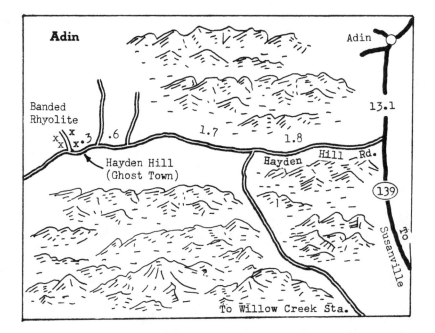

Adin

Adin

Banded
Rhyolite

13.1

x x
x x .3   .6

1.7   1.8

Hayden Hill (Ghost Town)

Hayden   Hill   Rd.

139

To
Susanville

To Willow Creek Sta.

Weathered house

HALLELUJAH MOUNTAIN

Hallelujah Mountain, or Peterson Mountain, as it is known locally, has been a highly regarded collecting spot for years. It boasts smoky, citrine, amethyst, milky and water-clear quartz crystals, some of which are rare scepter varieties. The crystals are found lining cavities in the country rock or loose in the soil of the lower slopes and washes. The most ambitious collecting method entails use of a sledge hammer, gad and/or chisel to split quartz seams in hopes of opening a crystal bearing cavity. This is exhausting work, but offers lots of potential. You can look for seams on the rocky ledges, high on the mountain or in any of the boulders farther down. For those not wanting to do heavy sledge work, good specimens can often be found by screening the soil in the washes and lower slopes. A good place to park and turn around is shown on the map. Be sure to close the highway gate after driving through.

Site B is only a short distance further south and offers fine jasper and occasional chunks of agate and petrified wood. Nothing is plentiful, but the quality helps make up for that deficiency. Start at the telephone lines and continue east quite a distance. Look everywhere, especially in areas of erosion. The jasper is generally in solid tones of red, yellow and orange, while the agate is primarily dark, with occasional interesting inclusions. This is a vast site, so plan to do some walking. Most of what can be found is small, but every now and then large chunks can be picked up. Once again, be sure to close the highway gate after you pass through.

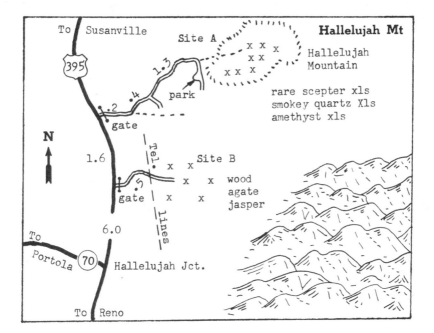

Collecting at Site A

CEDARVILLE

At Site A look for agate and occasional chunks of petrified wood on both sides of the ruts leading up the hill north of the main road. Pine needles cover most of the ground, so a small rake might be useful for exposing underlying rocks. The agate is generally white and clear with some containing nice bands. Most have an orange crust, however, so any suspicious stones should be split to determine their true identity. Contorted chunks of agate can also be found here, and these make interesting display pieces without being polished. Four-wheel drives can negotiate the road leading up the hill, but it is more productive to simply walk. Nothing is overly concentrated and most are quite small. Be patient, though, and you will find worthwhile quantities in a relatively short amount of time.

The road to Site B is washed out at the creek, but on the other side, continuing south for at least one-half mile, one can find more agate and petrified wood. The material is similar to that from Site A, but the concentration seems a little better, probably because it is necessary to walk rather than drive to the center of the collecting area.

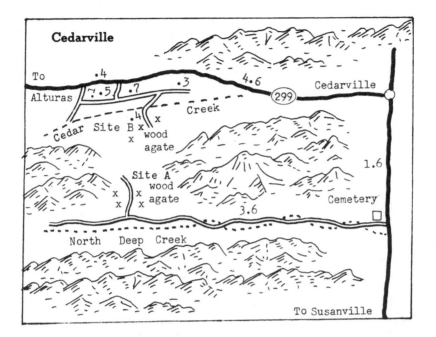

Wood and agate along Deep Creek Road

DAVIS CREEK

This part of California is one of the best places in the country to find gem grade obsidian. You probably won't need heavy digging equipment, since so much can be found on the surface. While working at these sites, always keep in mind that obsidian is volcanic glass and shatters easily. Because of that, collectors are advised to wear gloves and goggles, especially if they plan to split any boulders.

Site A is extensive, consisting of acres of obsidian-covered flatlands. Most is black, but some is a pleasing brown color. The quality and size varies considerably, with most of the gem material being somewhat small. Site B is similar to Site A, but the terrain is more mountainous and tree covered. There also seems to be a greater amount of gem material available. This site is centered around the intersection shown on the map, and continues for quite a distance in all directions.

Site C is the famous obsidian needle hill, and is probably the best known of these locations. Glassy needles cover the hill and it takes no effort to gather hundreds of them in a matter of minutes. In addition, one can find large chunks of obsidian, featuring beautiful double flow brown and black specimens displaying fascinating spotted and swirled patterns. Most of what is found here is gem quality and the quantity is unbelievable. At Site D, you must hike up a steep trail to the main digging area where specimens of rainbow obsidian can be obtained. Site E boasts more obsidian including a nice iris variety.

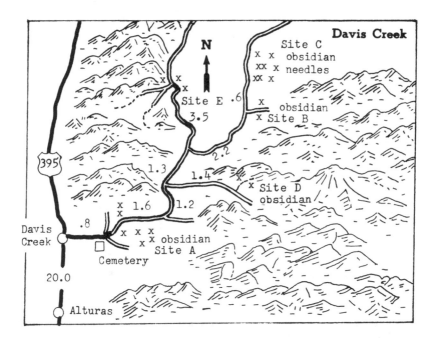

Davis Creek

Site C
obsidian
needles

Site E .6
3.5

obsidian
Site B

395

1.3

2.2

1.4

1.2

1.6

Site D
obsidian

Davis
Creek

.8

obsidian
Site A

Cemetery

20.0

Alturas

Collecting obsidian needles

LASSEN CREEK

Chunks of gem grade obsidian and specimens of petrified wood can be found at the locations shown on the accompanying map. At Site A, look on both sides of the road, especially on the hill to the south, for sheen obsidian. It is scattered all over and very little effort is needed to find it. The sizes tend to be small but a few boulders can be found hidden among the pine needles.

All the way from Lassen Creek to Site B, one can find more obsidian but the best collecting is done at the site itself. There you will see numerous pits where others have dug before, and it is no wonder why. This is one of the best places in the state to find golden, green, blue and silver sheen obsidian, as well as rainbow, black and mahogany varieties. Tons of material can be picked up from the surface, and, if you want to do some digging, nearly every boulder you encounter will be worth inspecting. The pick and shovel work is relatively easy since the soil is soft but be sure to wear goggles and gloves since sharp splinters can be sent flying through the air if you strike a chunk of the volcanic glass.

More obsidian can be found on the flatlands at Site C. This is an extensive area and continues for quite a distance in all directions. The final location, Site D, offers occasional pieces of obsidian and some very nice specimens of petrified wood. Collecting continues for about one mile along the road throughout the terrain on either side.

158

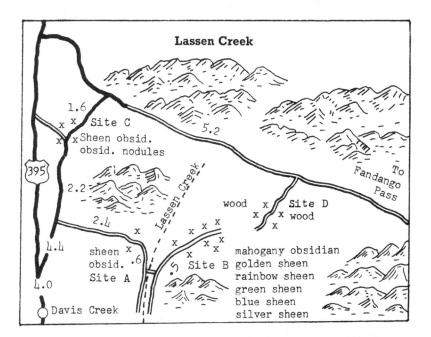

Lassen Creek

1.6 Site C
Sheen obsid.
obsid. nodules

5.2

395

To Fandango Pass

2.2

Lassen Creek

wood Site D
wood

2.4

4.4 sheen obsid. .6 .5 Site B
Site A

4.0

Davis Creek

mahogany obsidian
golden sheen
rainbow sheen
green sheen
blue sheen
silver sheen

Collecting at Site B